nizations should be designed for increased effi-
cy that will be of interest to the entire business
munity.

OUT THE AUTHOR

WILLIAM LORSCH is Assistant Professor of
anizational Behavior at the Harvard University
duate School of Business Administration. He
ived the B.A. from Antioch College, the M.S.
n Columbia University, and a Doctorate of
iness Administration from the Harvard Univer-
Graduate School of Business Administration.
ing 1964–1965 he was Research Fellow in
iness Administration and member of the faculty
Harvard. *Product Innovation and Organization*
awarded the 1965 doctoral dissertation prize
The program for *Studies of the Modern Cor-
ation*, Graduate School of Business, Columbia
iversity.

out the Program:

JDIES OF THE MODERN CORPORATION
Under the Editorship of Richard Eells

e program for *Studies of the Modern Corpora-
n* is devoted to the advancement and dissemi-
tion of knowledge about the corporation. Its
blications are designed to stimulate inquiry, re-
arch, criticism, and reflection. They fall into four
egories: works by outstanding businessmen,
olars, and professional men from a variety
backgrounds and academic disciplines; prize-
nning doctoral dissertations relating to the
rporation; annotated and edited selections of
siness literature; and business classics that merit
publication.

he studies are supported by outside grants from
ivate business, professional, and philanthropic
stitutions interested in the program's objectives.

Jay W. Lorsch

Photo / Vantine S

JAY W. LORSCH

Product Innovation and Organization

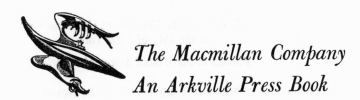

The Macmillan Company
An Arkville Press Book

THE MACMILLAN COMPANY, *New York*
COLLIER-MACMILLAN LIMITED, *London*

To Robin
who arrived with this thesis

STUDIES OF THE MODERN CORPORATION

Columbia University Graduate School of Business

The program for Studies of the Modern Corporation is devoted to the advancement and dissemination of knowledge about the corporation. Its publications are designed to stimulate inquiry, research, criticism, and reflection. They fall into four categories: works by outstanding businessmen, scholars, and professional men from a variety of backgrounds and academic disciplines; prize-winning doctoral dissertations relating to the corporation; annotated and edited selections of business literature; and business classics that merit republication. The studies are supported by outside grants from private business, professional, and philanthropic institutions interested in the program's objectives.

Richard Eells
EDITOR

Acknowledgements

In considering the various individuals who in one way or another have contributed to this study, I have been impressed by the fact that, although any thesis is primarily an individual effort, it nevertheless requires the contribution and support of persons with a variety of competences. I would like to express my gratitude to some of the many people who—through their suggestions, guidance, and often their own effort—have made the completion of this thesis possible.

One of the necessary ingredients for any research undertaking is financial support. In this regard, I have been most fortunate because the Division of Research of the Harvard University Graduate School of Business Administration, under the direction of Professor Bertrand Fox, has supported the work on this thesis, through a Ford Foundation Thesis Fellowship in Organizational Behavior, and also the larger research project of which it is a part.

Also vital in such a project are research sites that fit into the design of the study. The search for such locations was greatly facilitated by several individuals. Professor Ralph Hower made several helpful suggestions which eventually led us to one of the companies in the study. Professor Joseph Bailey and Mr. Charles Orth allowed me to interview participants in the Industrial Research Institute during the summer of 1963. These interviews enabled me to quickly locate possible research sites and, eventually, led to the selection of the second company in this study.

The executives at all levels in the two companies in this study could not have been more cooperative and helpful. Their frankness and their willingness to allow me to spend time with them were truly extraordinary. Perhaps only other researchers who have been involved in similar projects can appreciate the debt I feel to the individuals in both companies.

I should also like to express my appreciation to several individuals who have stimulated me intellectually during the course of this research and earlier. An interest in and understanding of the usefulness of conceiving of the organization as a social system was provided in seminars and numerous informal contacts with Professor Fritz Roethlisberger. Several of the specific ideas as well as a great deal of support were provided by Professors Douglas Bunker and John Seiler. I have singled out these individuals but there were many more, including my colleagues in the doctoral program and other members of the faculty of the Organizational Behavior group, who also provided suggestions, ideas, and guidance.

Mrs. Elizabeth Karpati and Mrs. Marianne Rusk have helped with the preparation of this manuscript in its various stages and versions.

Finally, I am especially indebted to two individuals who have been most important in facilitating the completion of this thesis and making it a meaningful and relatively painless experience. Professor Paul Lawrence, as the principal investigator in the larger research project of which this thesis is a pilot study and as chairman of my thesis committee, has proved to be not only an understanding administrator, but a stimulating teacher in the broadest sense of the word. His guidance and support during the past two years both prior to and during the course of work on this thesis have been a constant source of encouragement and stimulation and have contributed immensely to my understanding of man's behavior in organization.

My wife, Jo, has provided much of the emotional support which has propelled me through this work. As if this were not sufficient, she helped with many of the details connected with the completion of this effort.

Although all of these persons have helped to make this thesis a finished product, I, myself, bear the responsibility for its final shape and for any errors of commission or omission.

Jay W. Lorsch

Cambridge, Mass.

Editor's Note

Product Innovation and Organization by Jay W. Lorsch was awarded the 1965 doctoral dissertation prize by the Program of Studies of the Modern Corporation, Graduate School of Business, Columbia University. The dissertation was written for the Graduate School of Business Administration, Harvard University. The competition was nation-wide. The present book is a slightly edited version of the original work.

As an exploratory study upon which more comprehensive research might build, this material deals with the differentiation of organizations into sub-units and the integration of the activities of these sub-units to achieve a total unity of effort. While the setting of this study is two large chemical companies concerned with the development, manufacturing and marketing of plastic materials, the findings are applicable to any large complex organization, particularly those involved in transferring new technological and scientific knowledge into product and process applications. The author predicts the organizations with the major task of process and product innovation will be segmented into sales, production and research units and will develop integrative devices such as coordinating departments or teams to achieve the differentiation and integration required.

In the study three hypotheses about the processes of organizational differentiation and integration are tested:

1) If a coordinating department is effective in integrating

basic subsystems, it will tend to be intermediate between the basic subsystems in structure and occupational orientation.

2) Within any organizational system, the greater the differentiation between any two subsystems in relation to the requisite integration, the greater will be the difficulties in obtaining effective integration between them.

3) If other system characteristics are similar, the greater the degree of total differentiation within each system, the greater the problems of integration and the greater the dysfunctional consequences in system performance.

In conducting this research, the author has had to develop new methods for measuring the structure of systems and subsystems and the occupational orientation of personnel. Thus, in addition to finding new data and suggesting directions for future research, he has also made an important contribution to methodology.

Editor

Contents

i. Introduction   1

ii. The Research Setting   25

iii. Basic Organizational Differentiation   43

iv. Structural Integrative Devices   65

v. Processual Integrative Devices   89

vi. Differentiation and Integration in the Two Organizational Systems   127

vii. Summary, Conclusions, and Implications   149

Methodological Appendix   165

Index   179

Studies of the Modern Corporation

I
Introduction

This is an exploratory study of the functioning of two large organizations involved in the complex task of discovering ideas for new products and the improvement of existing ones, and of converting these ideas into products that are feasible and commercially acceptable. From a theoretical standpoint, the study focuses on the problem of obtaining task specialization (*differentiation*) for the units in the organization and of also obtaining an effective unity of effort between these units (*integration*). While the study has as a topical focus the problems connected with discovering new ideas in a research laboratory and converting them into marketable and producible products (the *scientific transfer process*), there is little doubt that any complex organization, whether it be a bank, a retail store, or a manufacturing firm, is confronted with the same issues.

Any organization can be usefully conceived of as a sociotechnical system in which behavior is influenced by a number of interrelated variables, including the individual predispositions of members, social structure, formal organization, and the system's external environment.[1] Organizational systems are involved in constant transactions with their technical and market environ-

1. A detailed explanation of this conceptual framework is given in G. Homans, *The Human Group* (New York, Harcourt, Brace & Co., 1950). A modified and more concise statement is presented in P. Lawrence et al., *Organizational Behavior and Administration* (Homewood, Ill., Richard D. Irwin, 1961), pp. 213–222, 534–546.

1

ment, and the strategy adopted to cope with this environment becomes the organization's primary task.[2] Each system has a number of units that can be conceived of as socio-technical subsystems. Behavior in each of these units is influenced not only by its structure and the predisposition of members, but also by the internal environment of the system of which it is a unit and by the external market and technical environment with which it must cope.

As the system develops strategies to cope with its external environment, these subsystems become differentiated around specific tasks designed to deal with particular sectors of the total external environment. If the system is to be effective in performing its overall task, a means must be provided to integrate the activities of these differentiated subsystems. The relationship between these twin processes of differentiation and integration is the theoretical focus of this study.

Since the publication of *Management and the Worker*,[3] which was the first attempt to study an organization as a social system, there have been a steadily increasing number of studies investigating many aspects of man's relationship to his organizational environment.[4] These studies have covered such diverse topics as work-group behavior, career development, and man's relation to technology; they have contributed to an increasing knowledge about the psychological and social factors that influence behavior in organizational systems. One area, however, in which there has

2. This topic is dealt with in a paper entitled "Socio-Technical Systems" delivered by E. L. Trist at an open university lecture jointly sponsored by the Departments of Engineering and Psychology at Cambridge University, Nov. 10, 1958. A further development of these ideas is available in A. K. Rice, *The Enterprise and its Environment* (London, Tavistock Publications, 1963).

3. F. Roethlisberger and W. Dickson, *Management and the Worker* (Cambridge, Harvard University Press, 1939).

4. Three such studies are: L. Barnes, *Organizational Systems and Engineering Groups* (Boston, Harvard Business School, 1960); H. A. Sheperd, "Patterns of Organization for Applied Research and Development," *Journal of Business* (January, 1956), pp. 52–58; R. Hower, and C. Orth, *Managers and Scientists* (Boston, Harvard Business School, 1963).

been limited research is the study of the process of differentiation and integration in large, complex systems.

Problems in obtaining effective working relationships between different departments in an organization are a constant source of concern to administrators, and there have been few studies on this subject. There appears to be a real need, however, to gain additional understanding of the conditions under which effective collaboration between different departments is possible. An increased understanding of the nature of these twin processes and their interrelationship would make not only a theoretical contribution, but also might make it possible to state more precisely how organizations should be designed to enable systems to attain optimal integration while still permitting their parts to be specialized in performing particular parts of the organizational task.

This theoretical focus is closely related to the reasons for selecting the topical focus of scientific transfer. In no other setting do the problems of obtaining effective integration seem more acute than around the development of products. It is a task that requires the close cooperation of research scientists, production engineers, market planners, and sales personnel if it is to be accomplished successfully. Behind these basic functions are financial analysts, purchasing specialists, quality control experts, and so forth, who are required to cooperate in providing various services. All of the personnel who must collaborate in this work are also representatives of highly specialized units, so that there is both a high degree of differentiation and a need for a high degree of integration. Thus organizations involved in the development of new products, as a central part of their total task, provide an exceptional opportunity to examine the problems associated with differentiation and integration which confront any large, complex organization.

At the outset of this project we recognized that in many respects we were venturing into uncharted waters where prior knowledge was limited and, in some cases, only suggestive. It seemed necessary, therefore, as a first step in any larger research undertaking, to begin with an exploratory study that would examine some hypotheses based on the prior research knowledge, would test these prior findings in a systematic manner, and would seek those emergent findings that could be more systematically studied in later research.

Although there has not been a large amount of prior research into the question of differentiation and integration in large organizational systems, this does not imply that this study is being initiated *de novo,* but rather that we are attempting to confirm and build on several different bodies of research related to the focus of this study. First, there are those few research studies and theoretical articles that have dealt with differentiation and integration in large systems. There is also a growing body of research on the relationship between the task of an organization and its structure. Finally, there are studies that have focused on the values of different occupational groups, as well as several studies examining the phenomena of intergroup relations.

Earlier Research On Integration and Differentiation

Problems of integration and differentiation are not unfamiliar to social scientists. As early as the turn of the century, Herbert Spencer pointed to the tendency for both differentiation and integration to be present in any social system:

> A social organism is like an individual organism in these essential traits; that it grows; that while growing it becomes more complex; that while becoming more complex, its parts acquire increasing mutual interdependence; that its life is immense in length compared with the lives of its component units; . . . that in both cases there is increasing integration accompanied by increasing heterogeneity.[5]

5. Herbert Spencer, *Autobiography* (New York, 1904), II, p. 56.

Spencer also indicated that the dual process of differentiation and integration occurred in social systems of any size, from a society as a whole down to the individual firm.

Elton Mayo, writing a half-century later, made a similar point:

> Every social group, at whatever level of culture, must face and clearly state two perpetual and recurrent problems of administration. It must secure for its individual and group membership:
> 1. The satisfaction of material and economic needs.
> 2. The maintenance of spontaneous cooperation throughout the organization.[6]

Mayo concentrated on the problems of maintaining cooperation, but the first problem is related to the second, in that the satisfaction of material needs has created increased specialization in organizations and this specialization (differentiation) is related to problems of obtaining cooperation (integration). This point is made quite clearly by Chester Barnard:

> Thus, in an important aspect, 'organization' and 'specialization' are synonyms. The ends of cooperation cannot be accomplished without specialization. The coordination implied is a functional aspect of organization. This function is to correlate the efforts of individuals in such a way with the conditions of the cooperative effort as a whole that purpose may be accomplished.[7]

Barnard goes on to point out that each unit in the organization is a specialization, and that the overall purpose or task of the organization must be broken down into unit tasks. One of the functions of the executive is to integrate the differentiated tasks of these units.

The need for specialization or differentiation occurs as the system attempts to perform the tasks required to cope with its external environment. But this differentiation makes it increasingly necessary to obtain integration of the parts of the system. These

6. Elton Mayo, *The Social Problems of An Industrial Civilization* (Boston, Harvard Business School, 1945), p. 9.
7. Chester Barnard, *The Functions of The Executive* (Cambridge, Harvard University Press, 1945), pp. 136–137.

references, and others that could be cited, indicate that the issues on which this study focuses are not novel, but the fact remains that only limited research has been conducted on differentiation and integration in organizational systems.

One researcher, A. K. Rice, who has examined this issue in complex organizations, points to the need for each unit or sub-system within the organizational system to be differentiated around a primary task if it is to be viable internally. This means that in complex organizations the differentiated subsystems will be performing discrete tasks, which must be integrated, if the organization is successfully to accomplish its mission. Rice makes this point in the following manner:

> For organization model building the differentiation of operating systems depends upon the discovery of sub-systems with discrete primary tasks. Successive orders of differentiation can continue until primary production systems are reached. Each differentiation requires a corresponding integration to assure that the primary tasks of the parts add up to the whole. . . . In other words, the viability of any grouping of sub-systems for command purposes depends upon the group having a discrete primary task that differentiates it from other groups of the same order of differentiation, and from groups at higher or lower levels of differentiation.[8]

Thus, on the basis of his research, Rice is pointing to the need for both differentiation and integration in large systems. These findings match the positions taken by Spencer, Mayo, Barnard, and others. However, Rice is also pointing to one phenomenon in the process of differentiation and integration which is peculiar to large, complex systems. As the task of the organization is segmented into subtasks, subsystems emerge with certain distinct characteristics that are related to their primary task.

Just what units an organization is divided into may vary somewhat depending upon the particular requisites of its environment, but it is apparent that there is a general tendency in all large

8. Rice, p. 225.

industrial enterprises for activities to be divided into three basic subsystems: Research, Production, and Sales. Wilfred Brown, in his description of the organization at the Glacier Metals Company, notes that these three major subsystems exist in any industrial organization. He describes their activities in the following manner:[9] 'They decide what goods or services they seek to provide. [Research] . . . They arrange for the provision of some good or service. [Production] . . . They arrange for the sale of goods or services.' [Sales]

In this study, then, the Research, Production, and Sales units are considered the basic subsystems in the organization. They are basic in the sense that, as Brown has pointed out, they are performing the major activities of the firm. The other subsystems that may exist in an enterprise have the function of controlling, servicing, or integrating these three basic functions.

The Dimensions of Differentiation

Up to this point differentiation has been discussed as if it only involved segmenting the organizational task into the tasks of subsidiary units, but previous research studies suggest that we can expect these units to also be differentiated along other dimensions. First, different organizational structures may emerge within each subsystem in relation to their different tasks. These different structures will influence norms and behavior within each unit. Second, other differences in cognitive states and norms may be expected to evolve in relation to the similar professional backgrounds and shared activities of members of one subsystem who are performing a common task. This second type of difference will be referred to as occupational orientation.

9. Wilfred Brown, *Exploration in Management* (London, Heinemann, 1960), pp. 143–145.

RESEARCH INTO THE RELATIONSHIP OF TASK AND STRUCTURE

Much of the research on this topic has concentrated on the functionality of different structural patterns for the performance of different tasks and on the tendency for systems or subsystems with similar tasks to have similar organizational structures. Rather than conceiving of all organizational structures as being identical and imposing the same constraints and opportunities, we now have research data indicating that there are variations among structures within the same system and between different systems and that these different structures tend to be suitable for different tasks.

Hints of a relationship between effective performance of tasks and the structure of the system performing the task can be found in several early experimental studies. For example, Leavitt, building on the earlier work of Bavelas with communication nets in small groups, found that wheel networks in which there was a central coordinating person could more effectively perform a routine task than circle nets where every person communicated only with his two neighbors.[10] Macy, Christie, and Luce conducted an experiment using the same networks and the same-sized groups as Leavitt but with increased complexity of the task.[11] In this experiment they found that the circle net seemed to perform better than the wheel on a complex task.

From these experimental studies we begin to get an indication that a more highly structured pattern such as a wheel network is more effective for performing simple tasks, while a less structured network such as the circle is more effective for complicated tasks. Leavitt, himself, has noted the implications of these findings for real organizational structures:

10. H. J. Leavitt, "Some Effects of Certain Communications Patterns on Group Performance" in Readings in Social Psychology, ed. Macoby et al. (New York, Holt, Rinehart & Winston, 1958), pp. 546–563.
11. J. Macy, L. Christie, and K. Luce, "Coding Noise in Task Oriented Groups," Journal of Abnormal and Social Psychology, XL (1953), pp. 401–409.

One cannot overlook, in this discussion of structure, the implications of the research on communication networks and other recent related work. *Direct* application of this laboratory research to the real world is scarce, though it has had some significant indirect influence on structural planning. In that research, variations in communications nets effect both routine and novel task performance rather significantly. The results suggest that appropriate communications structures might vary considerably within a complex organization depending upon the type of task that any subunit of the organization undertakes.

Thus for programmed repetitive tasks, centralized communication structures seem to operate most efficiently, but with some human costs. For more novel, ill-structured tasks more wide open communications nets with larger numbers of channels and less differentiation among members seem to work more effectively.[12]

Further evidence of this relationship between task and organizational structure can be found in several reports of field research conducted in large organizations. Joan Woodward, in a study of the organizational structure of 203 firms in England, found that among firms involved in unit production, mass production, and those in the process industries, there were differences in such factors as the ratio of managers to other personnel, span of control, and number of levels in the hierarchy. Firms using similar technical methods had similar organizational structures. She also found there was a relationship between successful performance and the organizational structure of companies within each industry. Those firms which were most successful in their industry had organizational characteristics which approximated the median of the organization in their industry.[13]

The significance of Woodward's findings are twofold. First, she found support in field settings for the conclusions of the experimental researchers that there is a relationship between successful task performance and structure. More importantly, she also

12. H. J. Leavitt, "Applied Organizational Change in Industry—Structural Technological and Humanistic Approach," Carnegie Institute of Technology. Mimeo (to appear in *Handbook of Organization,* March, editor).

13. Joan Woodward, *Management & Technology* (London, Her Majesty's Stationery Office, 1958). See especially pp. 16, 24.

found a tendency for organizations to adopt a structure consistent with the requirements of their technology.

Burns and Stalker, in a more comprehensive report of research conducted in several English and Scottish firms, also pointed to the relationship between organizational effectiveness and structure in different environments.[14] They examined several firms that had been operating in relatively stable environments and that were attempting to move into the more rapidly changing field of electronics. When these enterprises were operating in a stable market and technical environment, they had developed a quite rigid and highly prescribed organizational structure, which the authors termed 'mechanistic.' As the companies moved into the changing environment, Burns and Stalker found that a looser and less prescriptive structure was adopted. This they termed 'organic.' They concluded that the firms that could not succeed in the changing environment failed because of an 'inability to adapt the management system to the form appropriate to conditions of more rapid technical and commercial change.[15] The authors also pointed out that neither the organic or mechanistic type exist in a pure form but instead represent a continuum along which firms can be arrayed. Finally, Burns and Stalker make the point that there is a relationship between the different organizational structures and the norms and behavior of members of the system. From this work there is additional evidence of a relationship between task performance and structure in organizational systems. Low structure appears to be appropriate for a changing environment (complex organizational task) and higher structure for a stable environment (routine organizational task). These differences in structure appear to be related to differences in norms and behavior.

14. T. Burns, and G. Stalker, *The Management of Innovation* (London, Tavistock Publications, 1961). See especially pp. 1–10.
15. Burns and Stalker, p. 5.

One other recent study provides support for the view that there is a relationship between organizational structure and effective task performance. Lawrence and Turner in a study just completed have found data which support their hypothesis that 'given certain specified environmental conditions, organizations which operate consistently along either mechanistic or organic lines will perform better in regard to both economic measures and employee satisfaction than inconsistent organizations.'[16] They amplify this general hypothesis in two more detailed ones that point to the relationship to organizational effectiveness of consistency between organizational structure, leadership style, predispositions of members, and the organization's task. This provides further evidence that organizational structure, as well as these other interrelated factors may vary with the organizational task.

From both experimental studies and field studies of total organizations, we have found a relationship between structure and different organizational tasks. Yet our central interest at this juncture is in the differences in structure that will occur within one system in relation to the different tasks of the various subsystems. We have already indicated that we expect subsystems to be differentiated in structure and Leavitt was quoted earlier as pointing to these differences. R. H. Hall has recently found evidence that there are, in fact, differences in organizational structure between units and departments and that these differences are related to the different tasks of the units.[17] Units performing a simple routine task tended to have higher structure than those performing more complex tasks.

On the basis of all of these previous findings, we can therefore expect units within any organizational system to be differentiated in structure in relation to their individual tasks. Further, we can

16. P. Lawrence, and A. Turner, *Industrial Jobs and the Worker.* (Manuscript in preparation.)
17. R. H. Hall, "Intraorganizational Structural Variables," *Administrative Science Quarterly* (December 1962), pp. 295–308.

expect these structural differences to be related to differences in norms and behavior between the various subsystems. Also we can expect various units to be more or less similar in structure and norms, depending upon the similarity of their tasks. Moreover, we can also expect there will be differences in the degree of structure between systems. These differences in total system structure may also be related to differences in norms and behavior between any two organizations. This is a matter to be considered in more detail subsequently.

RESEARCH INTO THE RELATIONSHIP OF TASK AND OCCUPATIONAL ORIENTATION

The term *occupational orientation* will be used here to denote the cognitive orientations and norms that arise within groups working on the same primary task. We consider the term to include three dimensions: the *orientation toward task, orientation toward time,* and *interpersonal orientation.* Although other researchers have not made this conceptual distinction, there is some research evidence that different norms and mental states do emerge in relation to the differentiated tasks of the various subsystems and the different occupational groups working on these tasks.

Rice, in discussing the discrete tasks of each subsystem, has indicated that there will be differences in 'leader-follower patterns' (which is one aspect of what we are terming interpersonal orientation) between the subsystems.[18] In an extensive study of a variety of field situations, Fiedler has found a relationship between certain leadership conditions (task structures, the power position of the leader, and the leader's affective relationship with subordinates), leadership style, and effective task performance. Under both extremely favorable and extremely unfavorable lead-

18. Rice, p. 15.

ership conditions, a managing, controlling leadership style was found to be related to effective task performance. With intermediate leadership conditions, permissive leadership behavior appeared to gain more effective performance.[19]

Fiedler's findings are relevant to our discussion if we recognize that leadership behavior is closely related to the wider interpersonal norms of the subsystem. Although Fiedler is focusing on individual leadership behavior and might find some individual deviation from group norms, we would expect that the leader's behavior would generally be consistent with the norms of the group in which he operates. The introduction of the other conditions in addition to the nature of the task makes us more aware of the complexity of the factors with which we are dealing. However, the important findings for our purposes is that organizational conditions, including different tasks, call for different leadership styles (and presumably different interpersonal orientations).

From both these studies, then, we can anticipate that the different tasks of subsystems will be related to differences in interpersonal orientation. We should also note that although interpersonal orientations are influenced by a variety of other factors, including the individual members' predispositions, interpersonal orientation is related to the structure of a particular unit. In a highly structured unit, other things being equal, there would generally be more directive interpersonal norms than in a less highly structured unit. We do not imply that this relationship will be precise or will prevail in all cases, but rather that there will be a tendency in this direction.

Whereas interpersonal orientation concerns norms about dealing with other persons, orientation toward both task and time deal with the members' concerns with particular segments of the

19. F. Fiedler, *Technical Report No. 10.* Group Effectiveness Research Laboratory, Department of Psychology, University of Illinois (May 1962). See especially page 14.

organization's environment. The task environment is segmented
into a market sector where the companies' products are sold, a
scientific sector from which relevant new information is obtained,
and a plant sector which determines the technical and economic
constraints on processing and production methods. The environment can also be segmented along the dimension of time in that
different basic subsystems are concerned with the state of the environment at various stages, ranging from the present to long-
term, perhaps five or more years in the future.

No studies have attempted to systematically isolate differences
in orientation toward time and task in relation to different subsystem tasks. However, two different types of research have indicated that we can expect to find such differences, as well as
differences in other values between the various subsystems. The
first type of research deals with values among different occupational groups. Barnes has summarized the major differences between the values of science and those of business:

> Scientists traditionally pursue one set of goals or values. Business-
> men seek another. The scientist tends to identify himself with man's
> search for truth and knowledge. He associates himself with education
> and learning as they fit the traditions of pure science. One sociologist,
> R. K. Merton, observes that this value exaltation of pure science pro-
> tects science from outside influences which would dilute or destroy the
> value system itself. Science's value system thus performs the function
> of keeping pure science sacred and independent. H. A. Shepard stresses
> the need for such a value system as a major stimulus for basic research.
> Pareto writes that 'the quest for experimental uniformities is an end
> in itself.' Finally, Florence Kluckhohn pictures science's value system
> as an alternative to, not a part of, America's dominant cultural pattern.
>
> In contrast to this value system business pursues the values of
> financial gain and material achievement. These goals explicitly or im-
> plicitly serve as the dominant goals for both individuals and corpora-
> tions. Sales, productivity, and practicality further earmark business
> and its value system. While this value system encourages both gener-
> osity and idealism, both can exist only within the boundaries of reason-
> able profit and business practicality. In a sense, business has adopted
> the notion of practicality as its own value, and the American executive

tends to respect its connotation of common sense, feet-on-the-ground realism.

Quite clearly neither of the value systems reflect reality in any exact way. Both represent belief and assumptions. Both are subjective pictures, not objective representations. Each sets up certain 'good' goals in life that people 'ought to want' if they are to identify themselves with the particular value system. To deny these goals is to choose another value system.[20]

We should note that Barnes is referring to values which underlie the cognitive orientations in which we are interested. The fact that these differences in more fundamental values do exist is an indication that we can expect to find differences in both task and time orientation. It should be remembered that the scientists in the research subsystems we are dealing with have chosen to work in an industrial setting, and it is therefore quite likely that their values will not be entirely those of pure science. However, these researchers will probably be much more oriented to the values of science than will the non-scientists who are members of other subsystems. Finally, Barnes is dealing with business values as if they were homogeneous, and at one level they are. But our interest is in differences in values and cognitive orientations that may exist between different occupational groups within the business culture; e.g., sales executives versus production executives.

Anne Roe reports several findings which indicate there are underlying differences between various occupational groups. For example, on the Allport-Vernon Study of Values she reports that persons in sales occupations tended to have significantly higher economic values and significantly lower aesthetic values than the mean of the wider population. Similarly, she found that physical scientists tended to have significantly higher theoretical values and significantly lower aesthetic values than the mean of the population. Extrapolating from this finding, we might expect that members of a sales subsystem would have higher economic values

20. Barnes, pp. 20–21.

and those in a research subsystem would have higher theoretical values.[21]

She also reports that on the Kuder Preference Record chemical engineers, such as those who might be running a production plant, tended to score high in 'dealing with practical problems, rather than imaginary or glamorous ones.' Sales occupations tended to be lower than the average population on this dimension of practicality. Chemical engineers tended to be average in 'taking the lead in activities'; salesmen tended to be above average on this dimension.[22]

Miner, using the Kuder Preference Record to examine power needs among occupational groups in one organization, found that sales personnel preferred activities dealing with power and authority to a greater extent than the average member of the organization. Manufacturing personnel tended to fall at the mean for the organization; research personnel fell considerably below the mean.[23]

McClelland, in studying the need for achievement of a group of American businessmen, found that of five types of business occupations represented in the study (general management, sales and marketing, finance, engineering, and personnel), only sales and marketing tended to have personnel with a higher need for achievement than the average.[24]

From all of these studies, then, we might expect that members of a sales subsystem would tend to have a higher need for achievement, higher economic values, higher power needs, and to be less practical than those in production or research. Members of the

21. Anne Roe, *The Psychology of Occupations* (New York, John Wiley & Sons, 1956), pp. 156–158.

22. Roe, p. 158–159.

23. J. Miner, "Desire For Power As An Organizational Variable," Mimeo, School of Business Administration, University of Oregon.

24. D. McClelland, *The Achieving Society* (Princeton, D. van Nostrand, 1961), pp. 266–267.

production subsystem would be more likely to be highly practical. Research subsystem members would be more highly theoretical and have lower power needs. This discussion is not intended to be exhaustive but rather suggestive of the differences
in underlying values and interests of the various subsystems. We
anticipate that these basic differences in values will also be reflected in different orientations toward task and time.

Dearborn and Simon have reported findings which support
this expectation. Using a case study as a projective instrument,
they found that a group of executives tended to interpret the
study situation in terms of their functional specialty. For example,
five out of the six sales executives saw the principal problem to be
a sales matter, while four out of five production executives perceived that the major need was 'to clarify the organization.' The
researchers summarized their findings as follows:

> We have presented data on the selective perceptions of industrial
> executives exposed to case material that support the hypothesis that
> each executive will perceive as most important those aspects of a situa-
> tion that relate specifically to the activities and goals of his department.
> Since the situation is one in which the executives were motivated to
> look at the problem from a company-wide rather than a departmental
> viewpoint, the data indicate further that the criteria of selection have
> been internalized.[25]

Studies dealing with intergroup relations present further evidence about differences in mental states and norms between departments. Lawrence and Ronken, in an earlier examination of
the scientific transfer process, focused particularly upon the administrative skills required to gain understanding among the
several groups involved, so that social conflicts could be resolved
to the extent necessary to overcome technological problems aris-
ing around the new product. They found that one of the factors
influencing these social conflicts was differences in assumptions

25. D. Dearborn and H. Simon, "Selective Perception: A Note on the Departmental Identification of Executives," *Sociometry*, *XXI* (1958), pp. 140–144.

(orientations), particularly around the task.[26] Seiler, in two recent articles concerning interdepartmental relations, reports that there were differences in norms and mental states between departments and that these differences were related to the effectiveness of collaboration.[27]

In summary, prior research about the dimensions of differentiation between subsystems leads us to the following conclusions: first, we can expect that these units will be differentiated in structure in relation to their task; second, they will probably be differentiated in interpersonal orientation, particularly in relation to different tasks and in relation to different subsystem structures. There are underlying value differences between the occupations represented in the various subsystems and they tend to have different cognitive orientations. This fact, plus the findings of two studies of intergroup relations, have led us to conclude that we can expect to find that subsystems will also be differentiated in task and time orientation.

The Relationship Between Differentiation and Integration

PREVIOUS RESEARCH FINDINGS

It should again be pointed out that few studies have systematically examined the relationship of differentiation to integration. To do so is one of the major objectives of the present study. There are, however, a few studies that have suggested what this relationship may be. Seiler found that the fewer shared norms and

26. H. Ronkin, and P. Lawrence, *Administering Changes* (Boston, Harvard Business School, 1952), p. 203.

27. J. Seiler, "Toward a Theory of Organization Congruent with Primary Group Concepts," *Behavioral Science* (July 1963), pp. 190–198; and "Diagnosing Interdepartmental Conflict," *Harvard Business Review* (September–October 1963), pp. 121–132.

values two units had, the more difficult it was for them to collaborate. In our terms, this implies that the greater the differentiation between any two subsystems in structure and occupational orientation, the greater will be the difficulties in integrating their activities.

One factor that Seiler's work does not consider is the degree of interdependence required between the various subsystems. When the organizational task creates a high need for interdependence, or *requisite integration,* we are predicting that a given amount of differentiation will create even greater problems of integration. We can thus summarize the basic relationship between differentiation and integration by stating that the higher the degree of differentiation in subsystem structure and occupational orientation in relation to requisite integration, the greater will be the problems of integration. We should emphasize that while this differentiation may be costly for obtaining integration, it is necessary for subsystem performance. The problem confronting an organization is to achieve some balance between differentiation and effective integration. The system if it is to perform effectively, must contain some device to facilitate integration. This point has been made clearly by Eric Miller:

> Role-relationships cluster around the sub-tasks; such clusters of relationships become potential sub-systems; and areas of less intensive relationships become potential boundaries between sub-systems. Clustering may be functional for sub-task performance, but the associated discontinuities between clusters may be dysfunctional for integrated performance of the total task. It becomes a function of a differentiated managing system to compensate for these discontinuities.[28]

Miller's position that integrating the differentiated subsystems is the function of management, is similar to that taken by Barnard and by Rice. However, there is also some evidence that when

28. Eric Miller, "Technology, Territory and Time," *Human Relations,* XII, No. 3, p. 245.

there is high requisite integration between subsystems, as in the firms in this study, committees, liaison departments, and similar devices are evolved to accomplish this coordinative function. These devices appear to provide more detailed integration of activities at a lower level in the organization than does reliance on a top management group alone.

INTEGRATIVE DEVICES

The existence of these integrative devices is obvious to anyone who has observed the number of committees and similar groups that exist around the new product functions in any organization. Burns and Stalker have pointed to another integrative device, that of liaison specialists 'whose job was to move across linguistic and functional frontiers and to act as intermediaries between the people getting on with a job.'[29] A further indication of the presence of such devices is provided in the survey conducted by Booz, Allen, and Hamilton.[30] They report a rapid increase in the number of new product departments in companies surveyed. These departments, which often have such labels as Technical Service or Market Planning, have the primary task of integrating the activities of the basic subsystems.

These integrative devices are of two types—structural and processual. Structural devices are major organizational innovations. They involve the differentiation of a separate unit that has as one of its functions the integration of the activities of the basic subsystems. The processual devices may be either temporary project teams or longer-term cross-functional coordinating committees, but in either case they provide the setting in which the process of integration takes place. Although it is possible that these devices may in time become an intrinsic part of the formal

29. Burns and Stalker, p. 9.
30. Booz, Allen, and Hamilton, *Management of New Products* (New York, 1960), pp. 26–28.

system structure, we will consider them as distinct from the structural devices because they always retain their primary function as the locus in which integration activities are carried out. There has been no systematic research into the conditions which influence the performance of the two types of integrative devices. One of our purposes in this study is to examine some of these conditions.

Examining first the conditions that we predict will be necessary for integrative structural devices to be effective, we want to consider the position of the integrative subsystem in relation to the basic subsystems. If an integrative unit is to be effective in linking the basic subsystem, we are predicting that it will have to be intermediate in structure and occupational orientation between the units it is intended to link. Such an integrative unit will have more shared mental states and norms with these units than the basic units have with each other and thus should be able to obtain a greater unity of effort between them. The integrative unit that is not in this middle position may be more similar to one of the basic units it is linking, but it will necessarily be more differentiated from the other units and this will limit its effectiveness. In the course of this study, then, we will attempt to determine the validity of the following hypothesis:

> If a structural integrative device is effective in integrating basic subsystems, it will tend to be intermediate between the basic subsystems in structure and occupational orientation.

In exploring the conditions under which processual devices might be effective, we have started with no *a priori* assumptions, other than what factors we are not interested in considering. We are not interested in examining the internal processes of individual groups in order to consider factors such as leadership behavior, the phases of group emotion, or role differentiation. Other researchers have considered, and are still doing research into, the relationship of these variables to group effectiveness. Rather, we are interested in exploring total system structure or norms to see how these may influence the effectiveness of these devices. Out of this exploration we hope to develop some research leads which will enable us later to examine more systematically the factors related to the effectiveness of processual devices.

HYPOTHESES ON THE RELATIONSHIP BETWEEN DIFFERENTIATION AND INTEGRATION

Even assuming the existence of an effective integrative unit, there will be a certain degree of differentiation between it and the basic subsystems. Also there will always be a degree of differentiation between the basic subsystems themselves. In each system we will attempt to test the validity of the following hypothesis:

> Within any organizational system the greater the differentiation between any two subsystems in relation to the requisite integration, the greater will be the difficulties in obtaining effective integration between them.

In comparing this relationship in the two systems, we will consider the influence of the intervening variable of differences in system structures and norms. As we have already mentioned, Burns and Stalker have found that systems with low structure tended to operate more effectively in a changing environment than highly structured firms. The authors suggest that in a mechanistic system there is more reliance on higher management for integration, and that in the organic type integration seems to occur at a lower level.[31] This difference and other differences in system structure and norms could influence the relationship between the degree of differentiation among subsystems and the effectiveness of integration of their activities when we compare this relationship in the two organizations. Thus we would only expect the relationship between the degree of differentiation and

31. Burns and Stalker, p. 11.

integration to hold in both systems if other organizational characteristics are similar. In comparing the two systems we are also predicting that system performance (in this study, the rate of product development and innovation) will be related to the effectiveness of integration. If a system is not obtaining effective integration where the need for it is high, we can expect that there will be dysfunctional consequences in system performance. Our hypothesis about the relationship between differentiation and integration in both systems can therefore be stated as follows:

> If other system characteristics are similar, the greater the degree of total differentiation within each system, the greater the problems of integration and the greater the dysfunctional consequences in system performance.

Finally, in terms of this third hypothesis, we will attempt to isolate any differences in overall system characteristics between the two organizations and thus to delineate more precisely some of the factors related to the superior performance of low structured systems in performing scientific transfer in a changing environment.

II

The Research Setting

Before beginning an examination of the data collected in this study, it is necessary to briefly describe the requirements of the task of scientific transfer performed by the organizations in this study, and then to describe the two organizational settings. Although the organizations selected for study were both in the plastics industry, and although the study focused on the process of scientific transfer, which is a major issue in this industry, the processes of differentiation and integration operate in all complex organizations, and it is our belief that the findings reported here have relevance beyond these two organizations or even the particular industry. Firms in the plastics industry were selected for study because they provided settings in which the problems associated with differentiation and integration would be clearly visible.

The Requisites of the Scientific Transfer Process

The Environment of the Plastics Industry

The plastics industry, as it is generally defined, includes firms involved in many different types of processes at many different market levels. For the purpose of this study we are defining the

25

industry as one which includes companies involved in the development, processing, and marketing of basic plastic materials that are converted into finished products or applied to them by other industrial concerns.

By defining the industry in this manner, we are dealing with a relatively uniform marketing and technical environment with certain fundamental characteristics. Firms in this industry are conducting business with customers who have complicated processing problems of their own and whose products also have characteristics that are frequently changing. It is often difficult for the basic producer to accurately assess the needs of his customers or to anticipate all their processing problems. There is, thus, a high degree of uncertainty about market facts. This becomes more apparent if this industry is compared with other large industries such as steel or heavy chemicals, where customers may require the same products for years on end.

Another source of uncertainty in the industry is the large number of products with which any one firm is dealing. Even within one product family it is not uncommon to have a hundred different products with a multitude of different applications. Each application may create several technical problems of its own, which also contributes to the high degree of uncertainty about market and technical facts. Uncertainty is also generated by the fact that all the firms in the industry are committed to research programs that are producing new and modified basic materials, as well as new knowledge about these materials. Consequently, modifications in competitors' products and additions to the relevant scientific knowledge also present a source of frequent change.

Thus, the milieu in which these firms are operating is a dynamic one with a high rate of change in both the market and the technical sectors and with a great deal of uncertainty about marketing and scientific facts.

THE REQUISITES OF THE THREE BASIC SUBSYSTEMS

Firms operating in this environment have generally segmented the organizational task of developing, producing, and marketing plastic materials into the tasks of three basic subsystems.

The first of these, the research subsystem, carries on the activities of exploring the relevant scientific knowledge (environment) in a constant effort to discover new products, new applications for existing products, process modifications, and so forth. Although in the general sense there may be a large body of existing knowledge about materials, any particular problem the research unit works on involves exploring the limits of this knowledge, either to apply it to a new use or to develop new knowledge. Hence, its activities are largely problem-solving in areas where there are only limited facts available. The scientific sector of the environment is one that is changing rapidly. Scientific journals produce a constant flow of new information about changes in basic knowledge. Trade journals, industry shows, and the informal flow of information throughout the industry keep the researchers advised of changes in the state of knowledge and in customers' products. The uncertainty of information and the changes in the environment are complicated by the fact that the long period required to convert an idea from the laboratory into a commercial reality makes it necessary for researchers to work on problems whose solutions may not be achieved until several years in the future. This, of course, heightens the uncertainty of their task; since it would be difficult enough to be certain about this environment at a given point in time, and to be able to predict its course five years or more in the future is much less certain. These factors that influence the certainty of the task of a research subsystem are summarized in Figure II–1; the criteria used are described in the Methodological Appendix.

The sales subsystem is involved in the market planning and

Figure II–1—Task Certainty—Typical Basic Subsystems

	Certainty of Information	Rate of Change	Primary Time Span	Total
Research	1	1	1	3
Sales	2	1	3	6
Production	3	3	3	9

Low score = low certainty
High score = high certainty

selling of the company's products. The market sector of the environment also has a degree of uncertainty which is attributable to the complexity of customer problems and constantly changing customer needs, as well as to the pressures created by the active innovation programs of competitors. At any point in time, salesmen have a general knowledge of market conditions, but the constantly changing conditions make it difficult to be certain of their task for very long in the future. To the extent that the sales unit is involved in market planning for the future, this does create a highly uncertain task. However, the primary activity of most sales units is to sell existing products, and this makes it necessary for them to deal primarily with existing customer needs and market conditions. Therefore, although the task of this subsystem is somewhat uncertain, as the table above indicates, it appears to be more certain than that of the research unit.

From Figure II–1 we see that whereas the tasks of both the research and sales units can be characterized as being relatively uncertain, the production subsystem is dealing with a sector of the environment where there is a higher degree of certainty. Its primary activity is to operate the existing production facilities. In general, there is a well-established set of facts and specifications about production processes, and the consequences of any change in process are highly predictable. The certainty of the task is also influenced by the fact that, whereas sales and research units are confronted with constant change, the production unit is usually required to modify its operations only when some new or modified process has been fully developed. A final factor that makes the task of the production subsystem more certain is the need to deal primarily with day-to-day plant operations rather than those of the future.

From this discussion it is possible to summarize the requisites for each basic subsystem. Research must be concerned with the scientific sector of the environment and must be primarily oriented toward long-range concerns. Its task has a high degree of uncertainty and we would expect it to have a low degree of structure and, other things being equal, a permissive interpersonal orientation. The sales subsystem should be oriented toward the market sector of the environment and primarily toward short-range concerns. Its task is more certain than that of the research unit; therefore we would expect it to have a higher degree of structure than the research unit and to have a more directive interpersonal orientation. Production must be oriented toward the plant sector of the environment and will be concerned most with short-range matters. Its certain task makes appropriate a relatively high degree of structure and a more directive interpersonal style compared with that of the other units. Thus, as prior research has indicated, if each of these subsystems is to perform its primary task effectively, there will be these differences in structure and occupational orientation.

REQUISITE INTEGRATION

So far we have been discussing the tasks of each subsystem as if they were independent of each other. Yet before scientific transfer is possible, there are several essential ingredients for product development, some of which must be extracted from the relevant environment of each basic subsystem. First, the scientists involved must have scientific knowledge about the materials they are interested in developing. Obtaining this knowledge is the task of the research unit. The scientists also must have an awareness of some need for a product with particular characteristics in the market. This information must be obtained from the market sector of the environment by the sales unit. Finally, the scientists must be able to develop a process that the production subsystem can operate to produce the material with the desired characteristics at a feasible cost. To do this, the production subsystem must furnish data about processing limits and the feasibility of producing the material in large commercial quantities.

Once the research unit has assimilated these imports of scientific, market, and processing data and has developed an acceptable material, the process of scientific transfer is only half complete. Research must then collaborate with the production subsystem in successfully producing the material and with the sales subsystem in instructing sales representatives about the characteristics of the new material and in solving problems related to gaining customer acceptance for it. This conception of the scientific transfer process is diagrammed in Figure II–2. This diagram is an oversimplification; personnel in both organizations continually indicated that, although this was the way things usually happened, innovations sometimes did spring from the research unit with little prior knowledge of customer needs, or even from the production unit.

Two salient factors emerge about the required relationship between basic subsystems. First, the scientific transfer process requires a high degree of integration between sales and research, so that research can be aware of market conditions and sales can effectively market new products developed within the research subsystem. Second, a high degree of integration is needed between production and research, so that the research unit can develop a feasible product and the production unit can adopt the new process and operate it smoothly.

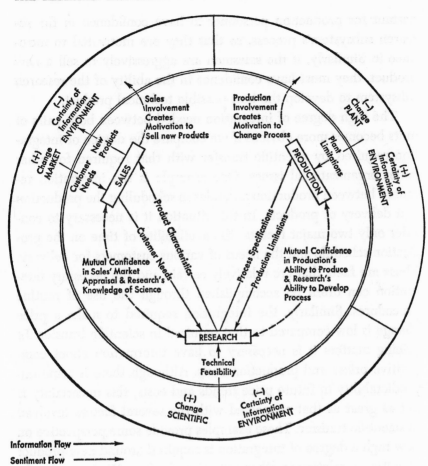

Information Flow ———————▶
Sentiment Flow ----------▶

Figure II–2—Scientific Transfer Process

These relationships are not only important because of the need for the flow of technical information, but also because a successful transfer requires members of both sets of subsystems to have a high degree of trust in each other and confidence in the outcome of their joint efforts. This is necessary if researchers are to work confidently on scientific problems without being distracted by concerns with the accuracy of market information. It is also important for production personnel to have confidence in the research subsystem's process, so that they are motivated to introduce it. Similarly, if the salesmen are aggressively to sell a new product, they must have confidence in the ability of the research subsystem to develop the best possible technical product.

The high degree of integration needed between both pairs of units becomes more obvious if we compare the degree of integration required by scientific transfer with that required for other major organizational issues. One example is the integration required between production and sales in scheduling the production and delivery of products. In this situation it is necessary to consider only two major factors: the availability of time on the production schedule and the needs of various customers for delivery. These are facts that are relatively certain and the necessary integration can often be accomplished through the use of routine procedures. Similarly, the integration required to make a price change is low compared to that required in scientific transfer. In pricing matters it is necessary to have information about competitive prices and production costs. Although there is some unpredictability in future price trends and costs, this uncertainty is not as great as that connected with the several factors involved in scientific transfer. These examples provide some perspective on how high a degree of integration is required around new product activities in relation to other activities of a firm. We have already indicated that the degree of uncertainty in the plastic industry is much higher than in many other industrial environments. This environmental factor is another indication of the relatively high requisite integration in organizational systems operating in this environment.

Thus far we have indicated that requisite integration is high between the sales and research units and the production and research units. In a sense, then, we have established the horizontal position of high requisite integration in these systems. Also of concern here is the vertical position in the organizational hierarchy of each subsystem at which high integration is required. We have mentioned earlier that other researchers have pointed out that integration is generally the function of higher management. In this industry, however, the complexity and uncertainty of factors in the market and in the scientific environment make it difficult for management at the upper levels of the organization to assimilate sufficient knowledge of the facts to effectively integrate the activities of the various subsystems. This uncertainty and complexity make it necessary for integration to take place at the lower levels in the organization where role occupants have the detailed knowledge of the market, of scientific facts, and of plant limitations which is necessary to make meaningful decisions that influence not only their own unit but other basic subsystems. This does not imply that no integration is required at the upper levels of management but rather that the intense, detailed integration between subsystems has to be carried out at the lower levels of management. Executives in both companies emphasized the importance of integration at these lower levels.

From this discussion there also emerges a clearer understanding of the factors that make the research, production, and sales subsystems basic. Each of these units has the primary function of coping with a major sector of the organization's environment. If they are not successful in carrying out a relevant strategy (their primary task), it will adversely affect the performance of the other subsystems and of the total organization. It is in this sense that they are basic units. Other units may emerge to control and integrate their activities, but without these three basic units effectively performing their task, no firm can successfully cope with its environment. If the basic subsystems are not effectively performing their individual tasks, no amount of integration can overcome this difficulty.

When we begin to analyze the data gathered in the two companies in this study, we will see some minor variations from the pattern of requisite integration described here. Yet we have set the stage for this subsequent discussion by establishing certain major requisites of the scientific transfer process. First, we have determined that the basic subsystems are required to have different occupational orientations and different structures. Second, we have indicated that a high degree of requisite integration is called for between sales and research and between production and research. This degree of required integration appears to be particularly high when compared with that required for other organizational tasks or with firms in other industrial environments. We also have indicated that the complexity and uncertainty of the environment make it necessary for this integration to be conducted at a relatively low level in the hierarchy of each subsystem. Finally, we have stressed the basic nature of the research, production, and sales units and the need for effective task performance by each unit as well as for integration. These requisites are the factors that we sought to hold constant in the selection of companies for this study.

The Two Organizational Settings

Several criteria were used to select research sites for this study. First the organizations were to be of such a size that their operation could be carefully studied—neither small organizations nor ones so large that a comprehensive picture of their functioning could not be obtained. Second, the two organizations were to be of approximately the same size. Third, the organizations should be operating in the same or similar market and technical environments. Last, the two systems should appear to have different system structures and norms. Although this last criteria could create difficulties in testing our hypothesis about the relationship between differentiation and integration in two systems, this risk was balanced by the opportunity it would provide to learn more about the influence of different system characteristics on differentiation and integration.

Individual plastic product segments of two large chemical companies were selected as being manageable in size. These were: the activities related to one plastic product family in Rhody and Procter Chemicals, and the Plastic Division of The Crown Chemical Company. These organizations also appeared to meet our other criteria. They were approximately the same size, and although it is impossible to find any two firms operating in exactly the same environments, these two organizations were coping with similar market and technical environments. Both were primarily processing products that were relatively mature as compared to other products in the industry. Although the two organizations were not direct competitors, they were selling products for similar applications to the same type of industrial customers. Both were seeking to develop specialized markets for their products, which required a high degree of customer service on technical matters. Because of these similarities we concluded that the external environments of these two organizations were as similar as we could hope to find.

At the time of our initial visits to both companies we obtained an intuitive impression of the degree of structure and the types of norms existing in each. Certain characteristics of the system at Rhody and Procter Chemicals seemed to indicate that a low degree of structure might be present. The executives with whom we met stressed the organizational traditions of individual autonomy and egalitarianism which they believed facilitated integration and encouraged personnel at the lower levels to make decisions and take action on their own initiative. The managers with whom this project was discussed also stressed a tendency to let the organization grow as the situation seemed to demand without being concerned with any of the classical management principles about organization or attempting to follow the traditional organizational patterns in the chemical industry. All of these factors suggested that Rhody and Procter was likely to have a lower degree of structure than many of the other firms in the industry and made it a particularly interesting candidate for this study.

On the other hand, our early impressions of The Crown Chemical Company indicated that it might provide the contrast we were seeking. Crown executives with whom we initially discussed the project were concerned because there was not enough reliance on what they termed 'informal communications.' By this they meant that personnel tended to rely heavily on the formal hierarchy for their communications with other units. They indicated that they were interested in establishing more direct contact between persons working on related problems in different units. Crown seemed to rely on more traditional management practices and had developed a system that on our initial visit appeared to be more hierarchical. All of these factors led us to conclude that Crown would be likely to have a higher degree of structure than R&P and thus would provide a good comparison.

These, then, were our early impressions of the two organizational systems, which only could be corroborated after we had completed the study. If they proved valid, we would have an opportunity to explore the influence of differences in system structures and norms on differentiation and integration. If after close examination they proved to be incorrect and the systems were more similar than we expected in structure and norms, we would be able to test our hypothesis about the relationship between the degree of differentiation and integration in two organizations.

RHODY AND PROCTER CHEMICALS

The Rhody and Procter Chemical Company (R&P) is one of the largest chemical manufacturers in the United States; therefore, to secure an organizational element of manageable size, we selected as the site for this study the research, sales, and production activities, as well as the integrative department activities, related to one definable group of plastic products. This family of products had a sales volume which was approximately the same as that of the Plastics Division at Crown. In this study, 'R&P' will refer specifically to those activities related to this particular family of products.

At R&P there were two different research subsystems—the Exploratory Research Laboratory and the Research Laboratory. The Research Laboratory had the primary responsibility for doing research on the product group with which we are concerned. Its activities were particularly focused on shorter-term applied research. The Exploratory Research Laboratory was involved in doing longer-range research of a company-wide nature, but this also included research on this family of products. Therefore, when we begin to discuss the basic subsystems at R&P, we will be considering four units: Exploratory Research, Research, Sales, and Production.

There were also several production plants involved in processing these materials, but it was not feasible to deal with all of them; we have, therefore, selected the one most centrally involved in processing new products. This plant, which will be referred to as the Production subsystem, was highly automated, although different products required varying conditions. The plant personnel occupied roles ranging from product section manager down to operators. In other subsystems salaried personnel at all levels were interviewed, but in the Production subsystem data gathering was confined to upper level personnel who were directly involved in product innovation.

There were two segments to the Sales subsystem: the headquarters product managers and the field sales force. Product managers were responsible for planning the sale of their group of products to a particular industry. There were three product man-

Figure II-3—Major Roles—Rhody & Procter Chemicals

Hierarchical Level	Production	Sales Headquarters	Field	Research	Exploratory Research	Integrative
1	Section Manager	Group Sales Manager	District Sales Manager	Laboratory Director	Laboratory Director	Group Manager
2	Plant Manager	Product Manager	District Plastic Sales Manager	Group Leader	Group Leader	Section Head
3	Production Superintendent		Salesman	Bench Chemist	Bench Chemist	Technical Engineer (2 levels)
4	Assistant Superintendent or Process Engineer			Laboratory Technician	Laboratory Technician	Laboratory Technician
5	Foreman					
6	Operator					

This chart shows only the relative positions of roles in each subsystem hierarchy. It does not imply that all positions on the same level have similar rewards, obligations, or formal status. The roles covered here are limited to those directly connected with the product group on which this study focuses.

agers and about forty salesmen involved in selling this group of products. Although it was not possible to gather data from all the salesmen who were spread across the country, representatives in one district office were used as a sample of the larger sales force.

In the Integrative subsystem, which had the responsibility for coordinating the activities of the basic units and for doing product and market development, there were three first level supervisors. Each of these three section heads had the responsibility for the development of products going to a particular industry and for coordinating the activities of the product manager and the group leader in Research, who were dealing with products for the same industry, as well as of the plant manager. (All of the roles in the various subsystems have been summarized in Figure II–3.)

The Crown Chemical Company

The Crown Chemical Company was also one of the country's major chemical producers. The Plastics Division in which this study was conducted was only one of several product divisions involved in plastic operations. However, it was the one that most nearly met our criteria for selection and provided us with the situation most comparable to that at R&P.

At Crown we will also be considering four basic units: the Sales, Production, and Research units, as well as the Exploratory Research Laboratory which reported directly to corporate management. The Research unit had primary responsibility for research and development of division products, including both fundamental and applied research. The Exploratory Research Laboratory was primarily responsible for long-range research that would lead the company into new product areas outside the scope of existing divisions. However, it also conducted research for the product divisions in areas in which its personnel had special competence or in which it had specialized equipment. In this

Figure II–4—Major Roles—Crown Chemical Company

Hierarchical Level	Production	Sales	Research	Exploratory Research	Integrative
1	Division Director of Production	Division Sales Manager	Division Research Director	Laboratory Director	Division Integrative Manager
2	Plant Manager	Regional Manager	Laboratory Director	Assistant Laboratory Director	Product Department Manager
3	Operations Manager	District Manager	Research Manager	Section Manager	Product Manager
4	Production Department Manager	Salesman	Group Leader	Group Leader	Technical Representative
5	Foreman		Bench Chemist	Bench Chemist	
6	Operator		Laboratory Technician	Laboratory Technician	

This chart shows only the relative position of roles in each subsystem. It does not imply that all roles on the same level have similar rewards, obligations or formal status. Roles above the division level have been omitted.

latter role, it was involved in conducting research for the Plastics Division, and for this reason we will consider it as one of the basic subsystems.

At Crown, as at R&P, there were several production plants, but to simplify the problems of data collection we focused upon the largest plant. In gathering data in the Production unit, we concentrated on the roles at the upper and middle levels, since these were the most centrally involved in scientific transfer.

The Sales subsystem at Crown was involved almost exclusively in selling company products and played only a minor role in market planning. The sales force was national in its coverage, but we concentrated our data gathering in one district office.

The Integrative subsystem at Crown was responsible for market planning and development as well as for integrating the activities of the basic subsystems. Its performance of the market planning function excluded the Sales unit from this role.

One feature of the Crown organization was that the Research, Integrative and Production subsystems were internally differentiated so that within each unit there were role occupants at the laboratory director (research), production department manager (production), product manager (integrative) levels who had the responsibility within their subsystem for a particular group of products. This meant the product manager had a counterpart in the other two units with whom he could integrate activities related to the portion of the product line he was responsible for. (The major roles within all of these units have been summarized in Figure II–4.)

From this discussion of the task differentiation in both organizations we can conclude that each had four subsystems that were basic and one subsystem that had the primary function of integrating the others. It should be stressed that although the same labels have been used for these units in both companies, there were some differences in their tasks. For example, the Sales unit at R&P performed market planning; its counterpart at Crown did not. The Integrative subsystem at R&P was involved in development work; this unit at Crown was assigned more of a market planning task. There were also differences in the tasks of the Exploratory Research units in both companies. The implications of some of these minor variations will become clearer in ensuing chapters. In spite of these minor variations in dividing the tasks of the two organizations, the basic subsystems in both companies had fundamentally the same tasks and for this reason we have felt justified in assigning common labels to them.

III
Basic Organizational Differentiation

In analyzing differentiation and integration in the two organizations, it is necessary to gain an understanding of the degree of differentiation that existed between the basic subsystems (production, sales, research, and exploratory research) without considering the integrative units or other integrative devices. This comparison is presented to demonstrate the differentiation that existed conceptually in each system and is not intended to be a representation of the situation in either company before the various integrative devices were created. Historically, the basic functional units did precede the integrative units and the other integrative devices in each company; as the integrative units were evolved, however, they were assigned certain peripheral tasks from the basic subsystems. This has undoubtedly altered the original complexion of the basic units. Nevertheless, examining the basic units as they now exist provides as close an approximation as we can obtain to the differentiation that would exist in each organizational system without integrative devices.

The Basic Subsystems at Rhody and Procter Chemicals

SUBSYSTEM TASK AND DIFFERENTIATION OF SUBSYSTEM STRUCTURES

On the basis of prior research findings, we expected to find that differences in subsystem tasks would be related to differences in subsystem structure. We further expected to find that these structural differences would be associated with differences in norms of behavior between the subsystems; this would contribute to the problem of obtaining effective integration between units. We also expected to find a relationship between the task certainty of the subsystem and the degree of its structure: the less certain the task, the less highly structured the subsystem would be.

The task requisites for the basic subsystems at R&P have been scored according to the criteria outlined in the Methodological Appendix: the certainty of information in the environmental sector with which the unit coped; the rate of change in that environmental sector; and the primary time span of concern of the unit. The less certain the information, the more rapid the rate of change, and the longer the time span, the more difficult it is to program activities and the less certain the task becomes. These data are presented in Figure III–1. One major distinction between them and the data presented for a typical set of units (Figure II–1) is reflected in the separation of research activities into two subsystems. We find that the task of the Research unit appears to be slightly more certain than that of the Exploratory Research Laboratory (ERL) because of the shorter time horizon of the Research unit. A second distinction between these units and those of the typical units described in Chapter II is that since the Sales subsystem at R&P was highly involved in market planning, it had a longer time span than our typical unit. We can expect to find that if these units are structured in a manner consistent with the requisites of their tasks, the degree of structure will be greater as we move from the two research units toward the Production unit.

Figure III–1—Task Certainty—Rhody & Procter Chemicals

	Certainty of Information	Rate of Change	Primary Time Span	Total
ERL	1	1	1	3
Research	1	1	2	4
Sales	2	1	2	5
Production	3	3	3	9

1 = Low task certainty
3 = High task certainty

The criteria used to score the degrees of structure in various parts of the organization (see Methodological Appendix) are: breadth of spans of control, number of levels in the organizational hierarchy, time span and specificity of formal review of subsystem performance, centrality to the task of formal rules, and specificity of criteria used for the formal review of the individual role occupant's performance. The broader the span of control and the less the number of levels in the hierarchy, the less structured is the subsystem. Similarly, the less central the formal rules are to the unit task and the longer the time spans of review and the less specific they are, the less structured is the subsystem.

Several facets of the actual structural characteristics of the basic units at R&P should be stressed. First, there was a wide range of spans of control, ranging from 4 in Research to 10 in the ERL. The differences in the number of levels in the hierarchy were quite small and probably had a negligible influence on any differences in structure. A more significant point is that there was no standardized reporting procedure for these activities. As a result there were some striking variations in the character and time span of formal review of the different subsystems. Results in the ERL were reviewed only quarterly, and review took the form of a seminar at which scientists presented their findings to their colleagues and the laboratory director. This can be contrasted with the Production subsystem, where, in accordance with the more certain nature of its task, reports were prepared monthly on a number of operating statistics. Rules and procedures covered only routine matters in the ERL, whereas they provided for almost all contingencies in the Production unit. Finally, the only prescription for the review of a role occupant's performance was that it be annual. The executive responsible for reviews in each unit determined the criteria to be used. These ranged from reviews based on several detailed criteria in the Sales department to a general discussion of overall progress in the ERL.

The individual characteristics of subsystem structure tended to co-vary (Figure III–2). As we expected, the ERL had the lowest degree of structure; the Production subsystem seems to have had the highest. This condition is consistent with the different task requisites of the two subsystems.

Figure III–2—Subsystem Structure Scores—Rhody & Procter Chemicals

Subsystem	Span of Control	No. of Levels in Hierarchy	Time Span of Review of Subsystem Performance	Specificity of Review of Subsystem Performance	Centrality of Formal Rules	Specificity of Eval. of Role Occupants	Total
ERL	1	1	1	1	2	2	8
Research	4	2	2	3	3	2	16
Sales	2	2	2	3	3	4	16
Production	3	3	2	4	4	2	18

1 = Low structure on this dimension
4 = High structure on this dimension

The Sales and Research subsystems had about the same degree of structure. It is difficult to make any clear distinction between these two units as to the certainty of the tasks, because Sales was involved with considerable task uncertainty in its planning function and Research was doing short-term applied research. In any case, there was some evidence that the degree of structure in Research seems to have been high for its task. This appears to be attributable to the fact that it reported to the Production Division, which traditionally had been highly structured. Although the members of Research did not indicate any particular dissatisfaction with this degree of structure, procedures were short-circuited to enable research to obtain necessary personnel or equipment, and this suggests that subsystem structure was not completely appropriate to the task. This is consistent with the findings of earlier researchers, which indicate that low structure is functional for the performance of uncertain tasks.

In spite of this one inconsistency between structure and task, we can conclude that the subsystems at R&P were differentiated in structure. Looking at the relationships between the two research units and Production and Sales, where requisite integration was highest in the scientific transfer process, we see that the structures of Production and Sales were highly differentiated from that of the ERL. While Research and Sales had similar structures, the Production subsystem was differentiated from Research (Figure III–3).

OCCUPATIONAL ORIENTATION

Beside differences in subsystem structure, we also expected that differences in occupational orientation would exist between the members of the various units. These differences in cognitive states and behavioral norms emerge in relation to the distinct tasks and structures of each unit as well as the predispositions of the different occupational groups. The greater the differences in these mental states, the more difficulties we expected to find in obtaining unity of effort between units. On the other hand, prior research has pointed to the importance for subsystem performance of members being oriented to the primary task of their unit. The three dimensions of occupational orientation are: interpersonal orientation, task orientation, and time orientation.

The different interpersonal styles in each department of R&P, as measured (see Methodological Appendix) by the use of the *Least Preferred Co-worker Scale* developed by Fiedler, showed a wide range of scores, from an average of 77 in the Production subsystem (which had the most directive interpersonal style) to an average of 112 in the ERL (which had the most permissive). Figure III–4 presents the mean interpersonal orientation of the four basic units at R&P.

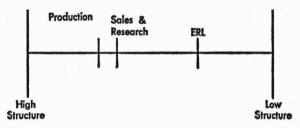

Figure III–3—Scale of Subsystem Structure
Rhody & Procter Chemicals

We expected subsystem structure and interpersonal orientation would tend to move in the same direction. A unit with low structure would have a relatively permissive interpersonal orientation, while one with high structure would have a more directive style. By comparing Figures III–3 and III–4, we can see that this proved to be the case at R&P. The ERL, with the least structure, had the most permissive interpersonal orientation, while Production which had the highest degree of structure had the most

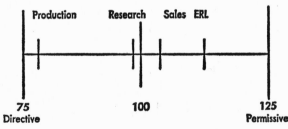

Figure III–4—Interpersonal Orientation—Rhody & Procter Chemicals

directive interpersonal orientation. Research and Sales, which were close together in structure, were also close in interpersonal orientation although Sales had a slightly more permissive orientation. Again, examining the relationships between the two research units and Sales and Production where close collaboration is required, we find that in interpersonal orientation the Production subsystem was highly differentiated from both research units, especially the ERL. The distinction between Sales and the two research units was not as great.

The second component of occupational orientation with which we are concerned in the various subsystems is orientation to task. The organizational environment was assumed to have three principal segments: the market, the plant technology, and scientific knowledge. The orientation of each subsystem toward these factors was measured in the manner described in the Methodological Appendix and these data are summarized for R&P in Figure III–5.

In orientation toward the market the Sales subsystem had a much higher concern with market matters than either research unit. The Production unit was the most highly differentiated with regard to production concerns. The research units with which it had to work to solve processing problems were evenly spaced in orientation to production concerns, although Research, with primary responsibility for these production innovations, was less oriented to production concerns than was the ERL. In research concerns the ERL was the most highly differentiated unit, followed by Research. Again the difference between these units and Production and Sales was quite large. Thus on all three dimensions of task orientation there was a high degree of difference in orientation between Sales and Production and the two research units.

The final component of occupational orientation with which we will deal is orientation toward time. Findings as to the orientation of the various units at R&P toward short-range (one to three months), middle-range (three months to one year), and long-

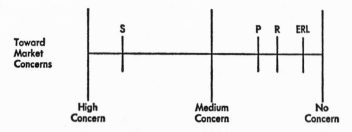

Toward Market Concerns

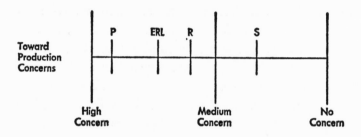

Toward Production Concerns

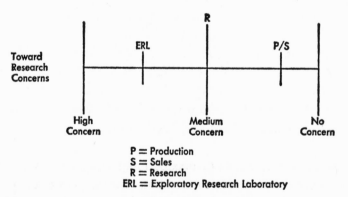

Toward Research Concerns

P = Production
S = Sales
R = Research
ERL = Exploratory Research Laboratory

Figure III–5—Task Orientation—Rhody & Procter Chemicals

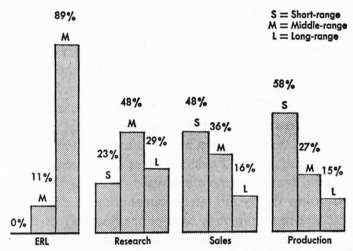

Figure III–6—Time Orientation (Per cent of time spent on problems reaching fruition in time period indicated)—Rhody & Procter Chemicals

range (five years) matters are presented in Figure III–6. From these it is apparent that short-range matters were the most important concerns of the Production and Sales units. The ERL was primarily concerned with long-range problems; Research, because of its work on applied and process problems, had a somewhat shorter time horizon and was primarily concerned with middle-range matters. Therefore, the major differences in orientation toward time occurred between the Production and Sales units and the research units, especially the ERL.

SUMMARY OF SUBSYSTEM DIFFERENTIATION AT RHODY AND PROCTER CHEMICALS

Since scientific transfer requires high integration between Production and Sales and the two research units, we will summarize our data about basic subsystem differentiation by continuing to focus on these relationships. In the structural relationship between Sales and the two research units, Sales was differentiated from the ERL but was similar to Research. In interpersonal orientation, these units were not highly differentiated. Sales was highly oriented toward the market, whereas both research units tended to be more oriented toward scientific and plant concerns. These units were also differentiated in orientation toward time; Sales was concerned with shorter-range matters, whereas the two research units were more oriented toward the future.

The Production subsystem was even more differentiated from the two research units. Production was highly structured; Research had a somewhat more moderate degree of structure and the ERL a low degree. In interpersonal orientation the Production unit was more directive than either Research or the ERL. The research units—especially the ERL—had a higher concern with science; Production was more concerned with plant matters. Short-range matters were the primary time concern of Production role occupants; members of the two research units were more concerned with middle-range and long-range problems.

In the relationships where there was a high degree of requisite integration, we have found differences in both structure and occupational orientation. As we have shown (Chapter II), this differentiation is important for individual unit performance but integrative devices will emerge where there is high requisite integration between differentiated subsystems. Therefore, we can expect that integrative devices will have been developed at R&P to facilitate the scientific transfer process between these basic units; these devices will be examined later in this study.

The Basic Subsystems at Crown Chemical Company

SUBSYSTEM TASK AND DIFFERENTIATION OF SUBSYSTEM STRUCTURE

At Crown, as at R&P, we expected to find differences in structure related to the different subsystem tasks. The complex nature of the tasks of the two research subsystems makes clear distinctions between them difficult; however, the differences in certainty between the tasks of the two research subsystems and the Production and Sales units are apparent from Figure III–7. The long-range non-routine nature of the research tasks should require more freedom of interaction between their members and less specific definition of activities than do the tasks of the Sales and Production subsystems which can be more highly routinized. Therefore, we expect to find less structure in the research subsystems than in the Sales and Production units.

Figure III-7—Task Certainty—Crown Chemical Company

	Certainty of Information	Rate of Change	Primary Time Span	Total
ERL	1	1	1	3
Research	1	1	2	4
Sales	2	1	3	6
Production	3	3	3	9

1 = Low task certainty
3 = High task certainty

The structural characteristics for the subsystems at Crown do not co-vary precisely, but there is a tendency for those with high or low structure along one dimension to have a similar degree of structure along the others (see Figure III–8). One notable exception to this tendency was the span of control in the Production unit, which was the broadest of any subsystem, while on other dimensions this unit appeared to be the most highly structured. Apparently, this contradiction was the result of the highly routinized tasks at the lower levels of the Production department. With highly defined procedures and rules it was possible to broaden the span of control without lessening the constraints of the structure. The other clear exception to this trend to co-vary was that the number of levels in the hierarchy was the lowest in the Sales subsystem, although this unit appears to have higher structure along other dimensions. The differences in the number of levels were so small, with the exception of the Production department, that this inconsistency did not appear to be important. It is worth noting in this connection that the Production department did have a much greater number of levels in its hierarchy than the other departments, which tends to emphasize its highly structured nature.

In spite of these minor deviations from the expected patterns, the two research subsystems tended to be less structured than Sales or Production. Thus we again find that the degree of structure becomes lower as the subsystem tasks become less certain.

Figure III–8—Subsystem Structure Scores—Crown Chemical Company

Subsystem	Span of Control	No. of Levels in Hierarchy	Time Span of Review of Subsystem Performance	Specificity of Review of Subsystem Performance	Centrality of Formal Rules	Specificity of Eval. of Role Occupants	Total
ERL	4	2	2	2	2	4	16
Research	4	2	2	2	2	4	16
Sales	4	1	4	3	3	4	19
Production	3	4	4	4	4	4	23

1 = Low structure on this dimension
4 = High structure on this dimension

Although structure was differentiated at Crown, it is important to recognize that many of these differences in structure were quite small. The spans of control in the different subsystems ranged from only 4 in Sales to 6 in Production and, as we have mentioned, Production was highly structured along other dimensions. Certain company-wide and division-wide procedures enforced a degree of standardization among the various organizational elements. Monthly 'Highlight Reports' outlining departmental progress were required from all departments. The division was required to use a standardized evaluation form for many role occupants because of a company-wide salary administration and promotion program.

Of equal importance is the fact that the subsystem structure as we measured it did not fit the task requisites of certain units. This was particularly true of the ERL which, although it had the lowest degree of structure at Crown, still appeared to be too highly structured for its task. This was indicated by the comments of several research managers in the ERL. One typical response to a question about how decisions to initiate projects were made was the following:

> When one project gets killed we get another one. This is a sore point with me because we aren't given a chance to look around ourselves for new projects. We are given a project and told to work on it. My objection is that we don't give the group leader and the bench chemist the time to investigate different problems before he is being thrust into a program. It seems to be a spur of the moment decision. The way management seems to think is, 'You are paying those people in the lab, so you have to do something with them.'

Another research manager in the ERL indicated that individual scientists found methods of avoiding the rigidity of the structure:

> The chemist can also initiate a program to a greater degree than the research managers would like to believe. It isn't always possible to get the control you think you ought to, because what's going on in a certain project is always linked somewhat to the influence of the man who is working on it.

These comments indicate that the structure of the ERL was so high it was constraining the creativity of certain scientists by restricting their ability to attack problems that their skills and interests indicated were important. The scientists had developed some methods for dealing with this high level of structure by informally changing the scope of projects; however, a lower degree of structure would have permitted them to bring their more intimate knowledge of technical matters to bear on the selection of projects. It also would have enabled them to perceive the limits placed on their activities as a consequence of commercial realities and not as being imposed arbitrarily from above.

There also appears to have been some inconsistency between the Sales task and the structure of that subsystem. We shall return to this shortly, but for now it is important to recognize that, in spite of these limitations on the degree of differentiation of subsystem structure at Crown, it did tend to vary in relation to the certainty of the task, and the subsystems were differentiated on this dimension. These differences are shown on a scale in Figure III–9. In the two relationships where requisite integration was the highest, there was a difference in structure between both the Sales and Production subsystems and the two research units.

OCCUPATIONAL ORIENTATION

The second way in which the basic units at Crown were differentiated was in orientation toward interpersonal style, task, and time. The two research units and Production were not highly differentiated in interpersonal style, but the Sales subsystem had a more permissive orientation (see Figure III–10). There is one apparent contradiction in these data, since we originally anticipated that structure and interpersonal orientation would tend to move in the same direction. Comparing the structure of the subsystems (Figure III–9) and the interpersonal orientation (Figure III–10), we find that this expectation is not substantiated by the

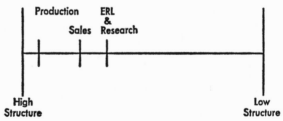

Figure III–9—Scale of Subsystem Structure—Crown Chemical Company

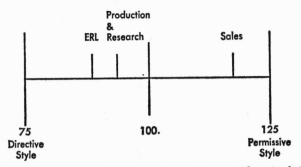

Figure III–10—Interpersonal Orientation—Crown Chemical Company

data at Crown. The ERL, which appeared to have the least structure, had the most directive interpersonal orientation, whereas the Sales subsystem, which had a relatively high degree of structure, was highly permissive in interpersonal orientation.

Several factors offer a possible resolution of this contradiction. First, as we noted earlier, some of the differences in structure between these units were not great. The differences in *Least Preferred Co-worker* scores for the ERL, Production, and Research subsystems were also quite small. These factors together with the small size of our sample in these units, especially the ERL, make it quite possible for a discrepancy of this nature to occur.

The inconsistency between structure and interpersonal style in the Sales department appears to be connected with the inappropriateness of the unit's structure to its task. Although Sales' task was not an uncertain one in comparison to the research tasks, it appears to have had some peculiar requisites which required less structure than existed in the Sales subsystem. In performing their activities sales representatives spent a large portion of time away from their supervisors and were only infrequently in direct contact with them. It was, thus, difficult for supervisors to exercise the same close influence over them that they could in a plant, laboratory, or office situation.

One indication of this is provided by the comments of a sales supervisor explaining how he short-cut the divisional policy that he was to handle all contacts between his salesmen and personnel in other subsystems:

> Sometimes, when I am trying to arrange these things (contacts between departments), I feel like an airline reservation clerk. It gets to be a nuisance trying to schedule our people and the technical people so I can get them all together at the same place at the same time. I get a little slack about having the salesmen contact me before they contact everybody at the headquarters or in the labs. Eventually you get to the point where you are just a middleman. In general my attitude is that if you are seeking or distributing information, talk to the other fellow directly, but keep me informed. All I want is to know about what they are doing before they do it.

This supervisor had developed his own device to provide more flexibility for the salesmen and to remove an administrative burden that was created by the need for latitude in a system too rigid in its structure in relation to both the subsystem task and the interpersonal norms of its members.

The interpersonal orientation of the Sales subsystem was not only influenced by the predispositions of its members and its structure but also by the customer. The customer appears to have been the most significant person in the salesman's work environment, and it is not unlikely that the Sales subsystem's interpersonal style tended to be primarily oriented toward establishing close relationships with the customer. Therefore, both because of evidence that the role occupants were circumventing the high degree of structure, and because the sales personnel had this high concern with the customer, it is quite possible that this permissive interpersonal orientation could have developed in a Sales subsystem that was more structured.

In spite of these inconsistencies between interpersonal orientation and structure, it can be concluded that there were some differences in interpersonal orientation between the basic subsystems at Crown. The difference which should be important in obtaining effective scientific transfer would be the rather large one between the Sales subsystem and the two research units.

The second component of occupational orientation examined was the orientation toward task of the various subsystems (see Figure III–11). In orientation toward market concerns, the Sales unit was highly differentiated. Of particular interest is the fact that the research units and Sales, which must work closely together to obtain scientific transfer, were widely separated on this dimension. The Production subsystem had the greatest concern with production matters and its orientation along this dimension was higher than the Research unit with which it was necessary to resolve processing problems. The ERL had the most concern with research matters, but it is interesting that it had less concern with these matters than either Sales or Production did with the factors which were their primary concern. This accompanied by the fact that the Research unit had an even lower orientation toward research matters suggests that a cognitive concern with research matters had not been highly differentiated. Even so, there was difference in orientation toward scientific matters between the two research units and Production and Sales. Thus, in each of the task concerns there was a difference in orientation between the unit with the primary concern for that segment of the organizational environment and the other units with which it was most interdependent in obtaining scientific transfer.

The final component of occupational orientation studied was orientation toward time (see Figure III–12). The two units involved in research matters were more oriented toward long-range concerns, whereas the Sales and Production subsystems were more oriented toward short-term concerns. The Research and Production subsystems had similar orientations toward middle-range problems, but Sales and the ERL were less concerned with these. As a result of these varying orientations we find that the greatest

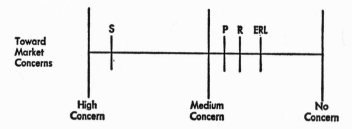

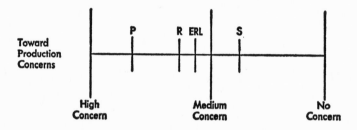

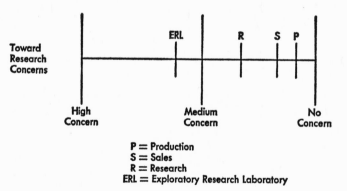

P = Production
S = Sales
R = Research
ERL = Exploratory Research Laboratory

Figure III–11—Task Orientation—Crown Chemical Company

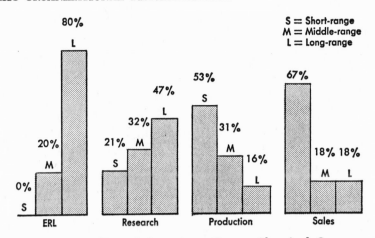

Figure III–12—Time Orientation—Crown Chemical Company

differentiation in time orientation occurred between ERL and Research on the one hand and Sales and Production on the other.

SUMMARY OF SUBSYSTEM DIFFERENTIATION AT CROWN CHEMICAL COMPANY

In summarizing our data about subsystem differentiation at Crown, we again have focused on the interdepartmental relationships with the highest degree of requisite integration—those between the two research units and the Sales and Production subsystems. Structure was most highly differentiated between the two research units and Sales and Production, with the latter units having a higher degree of structure. In interpersonal orientation the findings indicated that the research units and Production had similar interpersonal norms, which tended to be directive. There was considerable difference on this dimension between the Sales subsystem, which appeared to have a more permissive style, and the two research units. In task orientation the research subsystems had a lower orientation toward market concerns while the Sales unit had a high concern with these factors. Production and research units were differentiated in orientation toward production concerns. With respect to research matters no unit was highly differentiated, but the research units did have higher orientations in this direction than did Sales and Production. In time orientation the greatest difference existed between the research units, which were primarily concerned with longer-range matters, and the Production and Sales subsystems, which were oriented toward short-range time horizons.

Differentiation, therefore, existed between Sales and Production and the two research units in both structure and occupational orientation. Given the need for close relationships between these units, we can expect that integrative devices will have emerged at Crown to facilitate the scientific transfer process. Before turning to an examination of these integrative devices, we are now in a position to make some brief comparisons between the organizational system at Crown and that at R&P.

Comparison of the Two Organizational Systems

The data just presented tend to highlight several characteristics of the two systems, the implications of which will be considered in detail later.

In structure all the subsystems at R&P tended to be less structured than their counterparts at Crown. The average unit structure score at Crown was 18.5; at R&P it was 14.5. This difference was particularly noticeable in the fundamental research units. At R&P the ERL had a structure score of 8; at Crown, 16.

Structure also seemed to be more differentiated at R&P than at Crown. There was a spread of 10 points between the highest and lowest structured units at R&P, of 7 points at Crown. The significance of this is more apparent in a comparison of some of the basic characteristics of structure in the two companies. At

Crown the spans of control ranged from only 4 to 6, whereas at R&P they ranged from 4 to 10. Time spans of review of subsystem performance at Crown all tended to be one month or less; at R&P the ERL evaluated performance on a quarterly basis. The evaluation of role occupant performance at Crown was of the same specificity for all basic subsystems. At R&P one unit used detailed criteria, but the others relied on general evaluation. As a consequence, R&P subsystems tended to be more highly differentiated in structure than those at Crown.

In interpersonal orientation the subsystems at R&P were highly differentiated, ranging from a very directive style in Production to a permissive style in the ERL. While the Sales subsystem at Crown was quite permissive in interpersonal orientation, the other units tended to have similar interpersonal styles. Thus on this dimension also, R&P units tended to be more differentiated than those at Crown.

The sales units in both companies tended to be highly differentiated in market concerns. However, in both research and production concerns the subsystems at R&P, which had primary concern with these matters, tended to be more highly differentiated than the comparable units at Crown. In time concerns the subsystems in both companies had approximately the same amount of differentiation.

One final point about the higher degree of differentiation in structure and occupational orientation at R&P is worth noting. We have already mentioned that certain subsystems, notably Sales and the ERL, although highly differentiated at R&P, were more appropriately structured for their task requisites than the same units at Crown. Similarly, the occupational orientations of both research units and the Production unit at R&P were generally more highly differentiated than those at Crown, and prior research findings have indicated that this too would be functional for subsystem performance. From this we can conclude that the higher degree of differentiation between the subsystems at R&P provided a more functional relationship between task, structure, and occupational orientation than existed at Crown.

Two factors stand out from this brief comparison of the two companies. First, although the basic units in both systems were differentiated in structure and occupational orientation, the subsystems at R&P were more highly differentiated than those at Crown. Second, there was a higher degree of structure throughout all the subsystems at Crown than there was in the subsystems at R&P. As we examine the integrative devices in both systems, we shall be looking for any other differences in total system characteristics. We shall then consider all the differences in system structure and norms.

IV
Structural Integrative Devices

Differences in structure and occupational orientation did exist between the basic subsystems in both companies. For the process of integrating the differentiated parts of the two organizations we expected to find two types of integrative devices: structural and processual. The material in this chapter will test the hypothesis dealing with the conditions under which structural integrative devices will be effective:

> If a structural integrative device is effective in integrating basic subsystems, it will tend to be intermediate between the basic subsystems in structure and occupational orientation.

In discussing the differentiation of the basic subsystems, we have made several simplifying assumptions about both the scientific transfer process and the requisite integration in the two organizations. It will now be necessary to review the degree of required integration in each company, especially as it was influenced by the functions of the integrative structural devices. Therefore, we will first describe the task of the integrative subsystem and its role in the scientific transfer process. Then, we will examine the differences between that unit and the basic subsystems in structure and occupational orientation to see how the integrative unit is positioned among the basic subsystems it is intended to link. Finally, relying upon our clinical data, we will seek a tentative evaluation of the functionality of each structural integrative device for the system in which it existed.

The Integrative Subsystem at Rhody and Procter Chemicals

We have found that at R&P the basic subsystems with the highest requisite integration were highly differentiated in structure and occupational orientation. As a result we expect that a structural integrative device would have emerged to link Sales and the two research groups and to link Production and the two research groups. This was, in fact, the case. A separate unit had been established which had as one of its tasks the integration of the other units.

THE TASK OF THE INTEGRATIVE SUBSYSTEM

Integrative units also have certain instrumental functions which are related to their integrative role. The Integrative subsystem at R&P had two such functions: technical service to individual customers and the development of products. Besides this, personnel were expected to carry out the following integrative function: 'Coordinate their activities with other [Integrative] groups and with *Sales, Production,* and *Research.'*

Two levels of supervision were involved directly with the products with which this study was concerned. The group manager had overall responsibility for the activities in this product group within the Integrative subsystem. The section heads had responsibility for the customer service and development within a certain customer industry, and were responsible for the integration of Sales, Production, and Research activities related to products sold to this industry. Beneath the section heads were technical engineers, who worked on specific projects and customer problems.

Integrative personnel were required to work with field sales-

* From a departmental job description (italics added.)

men and the sales product managers in solving customer problems. In developing new products and improving existing ones, they were expected to work with scientists in Research and the ERL, keeping them advised of customer needs and obtaining their help in the solution of particular technical problems. The contact between the Integrative unit and Production was more complicated. Integrative personnel, by establishing performance requirements for new products, were expected to ascertain that the products which Production manufactured corresponded to those developed by scientists in the research laboratories. If products did not meet these specifications, Integrative personnel were then expected to work with Production and research groups to resolve the difficulties. It is important to recognize, however, that both Research and the ERL were also expected to work directly with Production in developing or modifying processes. This integrative aspect of the research task was housed in the pilot plant activities.

Relating this brief description of the task of the Integrative subsystem to our earlier discussion of the requisite integration in the scientific transfer process, we can conclude that the Integrative unit was intended to link Sales and the two research units, and Production and the two research units.

In considering the structure and the occupational orientation required for effective subsystem performance of the basic units, we were concerned with the environmental factors with which these units had to cope. However, although the Integrative unit did have certain instrumental functions, its primary task was to integrate the basic subsystems. In terms of structure and occupational orientation for accomplishing this task, the requirement if our hypothesis is valid, is that the Integrative unit be in the middle between the two research units and Production and Sales on all these dimensions. If it is in this position, it should be effective in linking these basic units.

DIFFERENTIATION BETWEEN THE INTEGRATIVE SUBSYSTEM
AND THE BASIC SUBSYSTEMS

The structural characteristics of the Integrative subsystem gave the Integrative unit a lower degree of structure than the Research Sales, and Production units, but more structure than the ERL (see Figure IV–1). Since the biggest differences in structure

Figure IV–1—Subsystem Structure Score—Rhody & Procter Chemicals

Subsystem	Span of Control	No. of Levels in Hierarchy	Time Span of Review of Subsystem Performance	Specificity of Review of Subsystem Performance	Centrality of Formal Rules	Specificity of Eval. of Role Occupants	Total
ERL	1	1	1	1	2	2	8
Integrative	2	1	2	3	1	2	11
Research	4	2	2	3	3	2	16
Sales	2	2	2	3	3	4	16
Production	3	3	2	4	4	2	18

1 = Low structure in this Dimension
4 = High structure in this Dimension

occurred between the ERL and the other basic units, the Integrative subsystem was in an intermediate position between the units that had the most dissimilar structures. This is illustrated by the scale of organizational style presented in Figure IV–2.

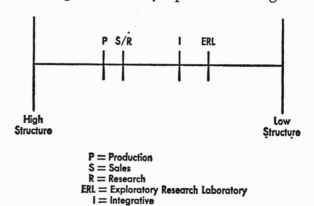

High
Structure

Low
Structure

P = Production
S = Sales
R = Research
ERL = Exploratory Research Laboratory
I = Integrative

Figure IV–2—Scale of Subsystem Structure—Rhody & Procter Chemicals

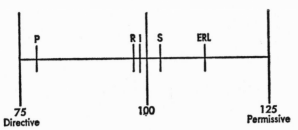

Figure IV-3—Interpersonal Orientation—Rhody & Procter Chemicals

Because the basic units at R&P were highly differentiated in interpersonal orientation, it was impossible for the Integrative unit to be more similar in interpersonal orientation to each of these units than they were to each other; however, the Integrative subsystem was intermediate between Sales and Research and between Production and the ERL (see Figure IV–3).

Task concerns were again examined in terms of differences in orientation toward market concerns, production concerns, and research concerns. The scientific transfer process requires high integration between Research and Sales, particularly in relation to concerns with the market. In this respect the Integrative unit was between Sales and the research units (see Figure IV–4). It is necessary, also, to obtain linkage between the research units and Production in concerns with production. Here, too, the Integrative subsystem was, to some extent, intermediate between the two units with high requisite integration. The Integrative unit's concerns with production placed it between Research and Production, but not between the ERL and Production. However, the difference in production orientation between Production and the research units was not large. In concerns for research problems the Integrative subsystem was intermediate between the Production and Sales subsystems and the two research units. Thus, in all three task focuses, the Integrative subsystem was nearer in occupational orientation to the basic units involved than these units were to each other.

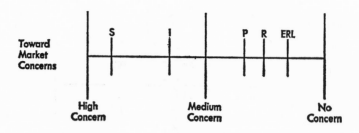

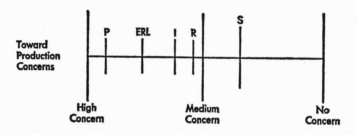

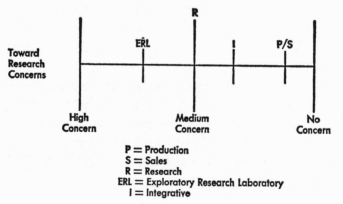

P = Production
S = Sales
R = Research
ERL = Exploratory Research Laboratory
I = Integrative

Figure IV—4—Task Orientation—Rhody & Procter Chemicals

Finally, the orientation toward time of the Integrative sub-system was compared with the basic subsystems (see Figure IV–5). The Integrative unit had a balanced time horizon, having been almost equally concerned with short-, middle-, and long-range problems. Because of this, we would expect it to be able to link Production and Sales, which tended to be primarily concerned with shorter time horizons, and the two research units, which tended to be concerned with middle- and long-range problems.

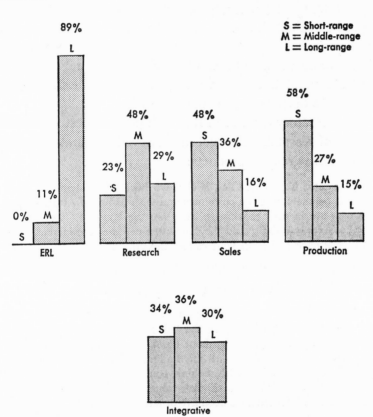

Figure IV–5—Time Orientation (Per cent of time spent on problems reaching fruition in time period indicated)—Rhody & Procter Chemicals

In summary, the Integrative subsystem appeared to be intermediate in structure and in all dimensions of occupational orientation between the basic subsystems it was intended to link. If our hypothesis about the effectiveness of integrative structural devices is valid, the Integrative subsystem should be an effective linking agent.

THE EFFECTIVENESS OF THE INTEGRATIVE SUBSYSTEM

The total spectrum of interdepartmental relations at R&P cannot yet be evaluated, but we can examine the views of members of the various subsystems concerning the effectiveness of the Integrative unit as a coordinating device. This data, can then be used to test tentatively the validity of our hypothesis about the effectiveness of integrative departments.

The laboratory director in Research perhaps best summarized the view of research personnel in the several laboratories associated with this group of products:

> The most important thing is that we have [the Integrative unit] with its contacts with the customers and with technically trained people who are in contact with us. They are the kingpins. They have a good feel for our ability and they know the needs of the market. They will work back and forth with us and the others.

The laboratory director in ERL expressed a similar view but stressed that this situation had not been achieved in a short time:

> I believe R&P has a good setup in the [Integrative unit]. They do an excellent job of bringing the industry problems back to somebody who can do something about them. They also do an excellent job of taking the projects out and finding uses for them. In recent years it has been staffed with, I think, competent men. Of course, the way it is working is an evolutionary thing and my comment today is different than it would have been five or ten years ago.

A group leader in the ERL was more specific about the value he derived from the Integrative unit's intermediary role:

> I look on [the Integrative unit] as an intermediary between us and Sales. I find it frustrating to be in direct contact with sales. What they [Sales] are doing is so alien to us that I'm glad [the Integrative subsystem] exists. The [Integrative] people we come into contact with we do have differences with, but these differences are no more than we have with our own research people and probably less.

Because Integrative personnel understood technical matters, research scientists apparently were able to deal more effectively with them. Sales personnel, who, because of the nature of their task, were primarily concerned only with marketing problems, would have had more difficulty establishing this rapport themselves. Further evidence of this can be derived from comments such as this one made by a group leader in research:

> [The Integrative subsystem] and Research are real close. I talk to them every day. We are usually together for long periods of time at least twice a week. [The Integrative subsystem] is on the border of research so we work together closely. The [Integrative] people are also just a step away from the customer, so when I make a change in a polymer I let him know because they may have a customer who can use it. The good thing about our situation is that [the Integrative unit] is close enough to Sales to know what they are doing and close enough to Research to know what we are doing.

According to research personnel, the Integrative unit was close enough to Sales to provide research with an understanding of the market, but was also sufficiently aware of technical matters to work effectively with research. The evidence indicates that the Integrative unit was effective as an intermediary; however, in maintaining a flow of technical information between the market and research and in establishing a sound affective relationship with the several research groups, there were also latent dangers in the research-Integrative relationship. Several scientists indicated that they appreciated the Integrative unit's role, as long as Integrative personnel only 'guided' research and did not 'direct' it. This semantic distinction, from the point of view of researchers, spelled the difference between the legitimate role of an intermediary unit and illegitimate initiation. Integrative personnel were aware of the potential dangers of encroaching on research prerogatives and apparently were usually successful at avoiding this pitfall. From the point of view of members of the two research units, then, the Integrative subsystem was generally effective as a coordinating device.

Most sales personnel also found that the Integrative subsystem was an effective intermediary. Their satisfaction with the situation was summed up by the comment of the group sales manager:

> There isn't much trouble between [the Integrative unit] and Sales. Some [Integrative] men aren't very good customer people, but if that happens we get them back in the [Integrative] labs and let them stick there. Some of our salesmen don't like to work with a particular [Integrative] man but that is more of a personal thing. Generally speaking, the feeling of close cooperation between [the Integrative unit] and Sales is echoed in the field. The top salesmen all get along well with the [Integrative] guys. You take a good [Integrative] man and a good salesman and that makes a powerful team. In our business the boys [in the Integrative unit] are topnotch.

The field sales force generally agreed with this appraisal. One salesman expressed it this way:

> [The Integrative unit] wants to know how much volume they can get if they make the research effort to develop a new material. We get into discussions about the worth of a particular product to R&P. But I would say this, [the Integrative unit] being reasonably close to the market is aware of the customers and they can evaluate things pretty well so I don't have too many differences with them. Once in a while I get a little annoyed because they want me to try a new product on a customer, when I have just spent six months convincing him to use one of the old ones. But all in all [the Integrative unit] is pretty sales minded so it is easy to deal with them.

Thus, from the point of view of sales personnel the Integrative unit was considered to be doing an effective job of working with them both on specific customer problems and in linking market needs to research activities. Because the occupational orientation and structure of the Integrative subsystem was intermediate between the research subsystems and Sales, Integrative personnel were able to understand and work with both scientists and sales personnel and were an effective link between these groups. The situation was perhaps best summarized by one of the scientists: 'The reason [the Integrative unit] is so effective is that they have two facets to their mirror; they can see both research and sales, while each of us can only see one facet.'

The other critical relationship where intense collaboration was required was between Production and research. Production role occupants also indicated satisfaction with the intermediary role of the Integrative subsystem. A plant manager explained how he was able to cooperate with the Integrative unit:

> An area where we can get into difficulty with [the Integrative unit] is around product specifications. We want specifications we can operate, although we know they must be acceptable to the customer. [The Integrative unit] would like them so narrow that the customer would never have any trouble. Usually what we have been doing is getting tentative 'specs' from [the Integrative unit] until we can work out our own. Once we have done this we give them to [the Integrative unit] to approve. I would say that we have such good relations with [the Integrative unit] that if specifications don't work out economically like we thought they would, we can meet with [the Integrative unit] and work out new specifications within our needs and the customer's needs. They always try to understand our problems.

Researchers involved in pilot plant activities and, consequently, in solving processing problems with Production and the Integrative unit also seemed satisfied with the latter's role in resolving these issues. One pilot plant manager put it in this manner:

> [The Integrative unit] are the people who tell us what the customer is buying, they get the prices and the kinds of material they want, and they, in a large sense, guide our research in the direction that has the greatest potential for product volume. These people are responsible for our success in being able to do this. Without [the Integrative unit] we wouldn't have been as successful as we have been in our ability to innovate new products.

Similar statements from other research and Production personnel working on processing problems also indicated a general satisfaction with the Integrative unit's linking activities. Since the Integrative unit was intermediate between both research and Production in structure and occupational orientation, this supports our hypothesis about the effectiveness of structural integrative devices.

In both relationships at R&P, where there was high requisite integration, we have found that the Integrative unit was considered an effective integrative device, and we have related this to its tendency to be more similar in structure and occupational orientation to each of the basic units than the basic units were to each other. The Integrative unit's structure and occupational orientation meant that its personnel thought and acted in ways that were similar enough to those existing in each of the basic units that effective working relationships could be developed with members of each of these other units. This tends to support our hypothesis that to be effective in obtaining intergroup linkage, an integrative subsystem would have to be intermediate in structure and in all dimensions of occupational orientation between the subsystems it was intended to link.

The Integrative Subsystem at the Crown Chemical Company

THE TASK OF THE INTEGRATIVE SUBSYSTEM

At Crown, the Integrative unit had been assigned the responsibility to 'manage specified product groups, by creating, administering and/or coordinating Research, Sales, and Production programs and to create new sales developments—be they product acceptability, prices, competitive activity, market trend, etc.'* These activities were carried out at three levels of roles in the department: the marketing manager, who was the chief executive in

* From the Job Description of Product Managers at Crown Chemical Company.

the department; two subsidiary department managers, who were each responsible for a broad portion of the division's product line; and several product managers, who reported to a department manager and were responsible for a narrower segment of the product line. There were also a few technical representatives, each of whom worked as an assistant to one of the product managers handling the major products. As has been indicated, the product managers had counterparts in Production and Research who were responsible for these activities for the same group of products.

One aspect of the defined task of the Integrative subsystem deserves particular attention. This is that its job was to coordinate the activities of the Research, Sales, and Production subsystems, but not of the ERL. The Research unit within the division had primary responsibility for carrying out research activities related to the division's products, so that the ERL was not considered to be an integral part of the scientific transfer process in the division. Any integration of its activities with those of other divisional units was to be obtained by the Research subsystem, particularly its higher echelons or the general management of the division. In considering the degree of required integration at Crown, we have to recognize that management had defined the highest integration as that being required between divisional Research and Production and Sales. Therefore, for the present the consequences of formally excluding the ERL from an intimate role in the innovation process in the division will not be considered. The focus will remain on the performance of the Integrative unit as a linking device between the Sales, Production, and Research subsystems. However, we will also examine the differences that exist between these units and the ERL, so that later the functionality of this arrangement can be studied. We should note, too, that the Research subsystem was also expected to perform an integrative function with the Production subsystem; this will also be dealt with in subsequent chapters.

Integrative personnel at Crown coordinated with the appropriate laboratory director three different types of research and development activities: those related to basic research, those intended to provide more direct and immediate technical service to the customer, and those aimed at improving present processes or developing new ones. They also had the responsibility of coordinating with Sales, Research, and Production 'policies and programs designed to maintain all operating staffs at a high level of product and industry awareness.'*

These were the major activities of the Integrative unit in relation to innovation, but they also coordinated such matters as scheduling and inventory levels between Production and Sales. Further, they were involved in establishing prices for products, in advertising and promotion policies, and in carrying on other activities that contributed to the sales of the group of products for which the individual managers were responsible. This included working with salesmen and advising them on problems with particular products and customers.

Since the primary task of the Integrative unit was to integrate the activities of Research on the one hand, and Sales and Production on the other, its requisite structure and occupational orientation, like its counterpart at R&P, was a function of the internal organizational environment and not of any particular sector of the external environment. According to our hypothesis, if this unit is to be effective in performing its task, it will be in the middle in structure and in each dimension of occupational orientation between the basic subsystems it is linking.

Differentiation between the Integrative Subsystem and the Basic Subsystems

Before comparing the Integrative subsystem with the other units along the dimension of structure, we should reiterate the

* From departmental job description.

point that the differences between subsystems at Crown in some characteristics of structure were relatively minor, owing to a tendency to standardize certain procedures throughout the division. However, the scores of structural characteristics for the several subsystems can still be compared (Figure IV–6). The In-

Figure IV–6—Subsystem Structure Score—Crown Chemical Company

Subsystem	Span of Control	No. of Levels in Hierarchy	Time Span of Review of Subsystem Performance	Specificity of Review of Subsystem Performance	Centrality of Formal Rules	Specificity of Eval. of Role Occupants	Total
ERL	4	2	2	2	2	4	16
Research	4	2	2	2	2	4	16
Integrative	4	2	3	3	2	3	17
Sales	4	1	4	3	3	4	19
Production	3	4	4	4	4	4	23

1 = Low structure in this Dimension
4 = High structure in this Dimension

tegrative unit is quite similar in structure to the research subsystems but is less structured than Sales or Production. Accordingly, the Integrative unit is generally intermediate between Sales and the research units, and between Production and the research units (Figure IV–7).

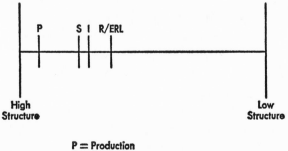

P = Production
S = Sales
R = Research
ERL = Exploratory Research Laboratory
I = Integrative

Figure IV–7—Scale of Subsystem Structure—Crown Chemical Company

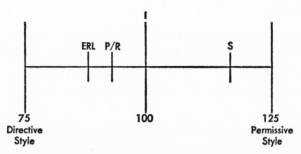

Figure IV–8—Interpersonal Orientation—Crown Chemical Company

In interpersonal orientation, the Integrative subsystem fell between Production and the research units at one extreme and Sales at the other (Figure IV–8). There was little or no difference between Production and Research in this variable, but there was a hiatus between Sales and Research. The Integrative subsystem appears to have been closer in interpersonal orientation to each of these units than they were to each other.

Turning to task orientation (Figure IV–9), we find that in concerns with the market the Integrative unit does lie between Sales and Research, and we would expect this to facilitate its role in linking these two units. On the other hand, in production concerns the Integrative unit is further removed from the Production subsystem than is Research, and we would predict that this would not improve its ability to serve as an intermediary between these two units. It should also be noted that the Integrative unit was intermediate in market concerns between Sales and the ERL, but was not intermediate between Production and the ERL in production concerns.

In examining the Integrative unit's orientation toward scientific concerns, we should first recall that only the ERL indicated a relatively high concern with these factors at Crown; Sales and Production seem to have been so low that there was still a gap between them and Research. Apparently, the Integrative unit did nothing to close the gap between Sales and Research, since it indicated roughly the same concern with scientific matters that the Sales unit did. Because the Integrative unit appears to have been somewhat closer to Research than was Production, this may have helped it work more effectively between these units.

In summary, the task orientation of the Integrative unit was intermediate between Research and Sales in market concerns and between Production and Research in scientific concerns; however, it did not close the gap between Production and Research in production matters nor between Sales and Research in scientific matters.

If the Integrative subsystem was to be completely effective as a linking unit, we would expect it to have a concern with time that would balance the differences in time orientation between Research, which was more concerned with long-range and middle-range problems, and Sales and Production, which were more concerned with short-range matters. The data (Figure IV–10), however, reveal that the Integrative unit was heavily concerned with short-range problems and had a very low concern with middle- and long-range affairs. According to our hypothesis, this would be expected to limit its effectiveness as a linking unit between Research and Sales and Production.

At Crown, then, we have found that a structural integrative device did emerge. The Integrative unit was created with the prescribed function of linking Sales, Production, and the divisional Research unit. We have found that the Integrative subsystem was not entirely intermediate between the units it was intended to link along all the dimensions of occupational orientation. In interpersonal orientation, the Integrative unit was intermediate between the basic subsystems. In orientation toward task, it tended to be intermediate in marketing concerns but not in production or scientific concerns. In orientation toward time, we also found the Integrative unit to be deficient as a linking entity,

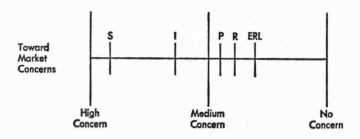

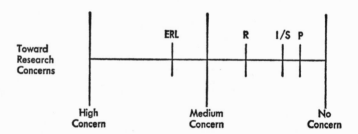

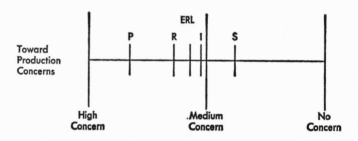

P = Production
S = Sales
R = Research
ERL = Exploratory Research Laboratory
I = Integrative

Figure IV-9—Task Orientation—Crown Chemical Company

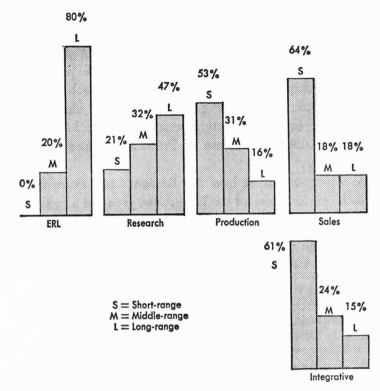

Figure IV–10—Time Orientation (Per cent of time spent on problems reaching fruition in time period indicated.)—Crown Chemical Company

since it had a high concern with short term matters and a very low concern with long-range or middle-range problems.

If our hypothesis about the need for effective structural devices to be intermediate in structure and occupational orientation is valid, we would expect that the Integrative subsystem at Crown would not be a completely effective integrative device.

THE EFFECTIVENESS OF THE INTEGRATIVE SUBSYSTEM

A complete evaluation of the state of integration problems at Crown is not yet feasible, but it is possible at this juncture to present some data collected through interviews about the effectiveness of the Integrative subsystem as a liaison device. As a result of our findings about the differentiation of this Integrative unit, and if our hypothesis is valid, we would expect the primary criticisms of its effectiveness to come from the Research unit, which was more concerned with longer-range scientific considerations. We might also expect Production personnel to find the Integrative subsystem insufficiently aware of Production concerns and behavioral norms.

We will first look at how the Research role occupants perceived the performance of the Integrative group as a linking unit. One laboratory director stated this opinion:

> My biggest criticism of our situation is that the [Integrative subsystem] isn't a good enough mechanism to link the research activities to the customer. We need a better marketing strategy on certain products and some long term plans. The lack of planning in [the Integrative subsystem] is deplorable. I am no marketing man, but I can see that one of our troubles is that the [Integrative] people are so tied up in day-to-day detail that they can't look to the future. They are still concerned with '64 materials when they should be concerned with '65 markets.

A research manager made another typical comment:

> The product manager is under a lot of pressure to work with the salesmen on existing products in our product line. What the product manager should be and often tries to act like is a liaison person, but in reality he is not. He is too concerned with sales problems.

A second laboratory director summarized the situation in similar terms:

> One problem is we can't get the technical problems the customer is having clearly defined. Theoretically the product manager should be able to handle this because he knows the customer best. But he is so involved in present business it takes all his time. He has a budget which he has to live up to and the best way to make money is to sell existing products. He knows that selling existing products is more profitable than selling new products, so he keeps on selling existing products to live up to the expectations of the budget.

These comments, and many others from personnel at all levels of the Research subsystem, indicate that the Integrative unit was not able to link them effectively to the customer's needs because the subsystem was too involved in short-term concerns and not enough with longer-term technical matters. That this situation could, to a large extent, be alleviated was indicated by comments from several scientists who worked with a product manager who had a reputation for concentrating on longer range scientific problems. The following comment is typical:

> The product manager's main function is to provide us with market information and market contacts. He also provides technical service and trouble-shooting in existing products. 'X' [the successful product manager] is basically technical so we work quite well together. Some of the other product managers are basically salesmen and they don't work as well. I think 'X' needs an assistant to help him on short-range matters. He is personally geared to long-range thinking, himself, so he is good at it.
>
> If these relations with [the Integrative unit] fall down I try to do something about them. If we didn't have an [Integrative] set up which worked well, it would compound our frustration. As it is with things working out well with 'X' it is just the day-to-day problems which cause frustrations. Your job and what people think of you depends not only on your technical success, but on your marketing success as well. As we get out products we get more dollars for people, equipment, and so on, from management and we are better able to do our work.

This comment not only points to the importance of maintaining effective linkage between Research and the market, but also indicates one possible reason for the difficulty of product managers in focusing on longer-range problems. All of the product managers had spent time as salesmen and many of them indicated that they still got satisfaction from this activity. As one product manager put it:

> I was in direct selling and there is nothing more thrilling than a big sale. Today I still get a thrill out of going out with a cub salesman and helping him push a sale when he is having trouble with a customer. I spend 40 per cent of my time doing this, usually on a

promotion of a new product. Once in a while you get a sale on an old product and that is when you really get a thrill.

Because the product managers found satisfaction in selling, and because it was consistent with their task of promoting the sale of products for which they were responsible, they tended to devote time to this activity. Their activities in dealing with scheduling, delivery, and customer problems also focused their attention on immediate sales matters. Thus they did not devote the attention to longer-term research affairs that the Research subsystem felt was required to provide effective linkage to the field sales force and the customer. When a product manager, such as the one cited above, was able to do this he apparently obtained more satisfactory linkage. At least Research personnel considered this to be the case. This evidence tends to support our prediction that the Integrative unit's effectiveness in linking the other subsystems would be impaired by its high concern with short-term problems and its lack of concern with scientific matters.

The low concern of Integrative personnel with Production problems contributed to difficulties in the Integrative unit's role as an intermediary with Production. One department manager in production indicated his dissatisfaction:

> The [Integrative] people want to get us into commitments that neither Research nor Production are going to be able to come up with. For example, on certain products the [Integrative] people want both heat resistance and better moldability. Well, those two things just aren't compatible. Sure, the customer would prefer a Cadillac instead of a Chevrolet, but we just can't give it to him. . . . Many of the [Integrative] demands, I don't think, are warranted. They don't give us enough time. They want to shift yesterday. I guess if I were in their position, where I had somebody hitting me over the head to sell, I would have promised the moon too.

Integrative personnel thought and behaved so much like sales managers that they were having difficulty establishing a sound relationship with production.

Thus, the task requisites and prior experiences of Integrative personnel tended to orient them toward problems of the market and, only to a lesser extent, toward technical and scientific concerns. These same factors seemed to create an over-concern with immediate problems instead of those in the future. As the following comment by a product manager indicates, some of them were aware of their dilemma:

> My position is certainly a liaison position. It is used to tie together what goes on in the technical areas and what goes on in the field. In many industries this is an unusual position. It is quite interesting, although you feel sometimes you are not appreciated enough on one side or the other. That is, the sales people don't appreciate the technical qualities you have and the technical people don't appreciate the sales competence you have. You are sort of the man in the middle. This position is essential for any outfit that wants to grow. You have to bring out new products and find needs in ways that are not impossible to achieve. A product manager is generally highly sales oriented, but he should also be development minded. This presents a terrific conflict between what you can sell now and what you can sell in the future. We should be concerned about the future, but often because of the current pressures we aren't.

This conflict that the product managers found in playing their linking role, along with the dissatisfactions expressed by Research and Production personnel, seem to be related to the differences in occupational orientation that existed between the Integrative subsystem and Research and Production. Because the Integrative unit was not intermediate along the time and task dimensions, it appears to have had difficulty in linking the basic subsystems of Production, Research, and Sales. The situation at Crown also tends to support our hypothesis that to be effective in obtaining integration, structural devices would have to be intermediate, in subsystem structure and occupational orientation, between the subsystems they were intended to link.

We have found, then, that structural integrative devices were present in both systems to link the basic subsystems that had high requisite integration. More significantly we have found that the effectiveness of these devices was a function of their intermediate position between the basic subsystems. This tends to support our hypothesis that:

> If a structural integrative device is effective in integrating basic subsystems, it will tend to be intermediate between the basic subsystems in structure and occupational orientation.

Although we have found this general support for the hypothesis, there is one interesting difference in the two organizations which we will want to investigate further in later chapters. The subsystems at Crown were not as highly differentiated as their counterparts at R&P; yet the organizational system at Crown appears to have had greater problems of integration than at R&P. One factor that accounts for this difference, and that we have been pointing to in this chapter, is the difference in integrative structural devices. The Integrative subsystem at R&P was differentiated in a manner which provided it with an occupational orientation and structure consistent with its integrative role. Its members seemed to share norms and orientations with the personnel in the several units it was linking. The Integrative subsystem at Crown, which was differentiated with a lower orientation toward research and production concerns and a short-range time orientation, was not consistent in occupational orientation with its intended function as a linking unit. Its members understood the problems of the sales unit but did not share orientations and norms with Production and research personnel.

Other differences in the system structures at the two companies were noted in the last chapter. These, also, were influencing the integration process. In continuing our discussion of integrative devices by focusing on those of a processual nature, we will want to begin to consider the influence of some of these total system influences.

V
Processual Integrative Devices

The processual type of device implies less commitment of organizational resources to the integrative process than does the structural type. Generally, such typical processual devices as committees and teams do not have the permanence of the structural devices, but it is possible for them to become part of the formal structure of the organizational system. Even in this situation we will consider these devices as processual because their function is still to provide the setting in which the process of integration is carried out.

The objectives of this chapter are twofold. First, we want to check our expectation that processual integrative devices will also emerge to integrate differentiated subsystems when requisite integration is high. Second, we want to examine the conditions in both organizations which tended to make processual devices effective for obtaining linkage. To accomplish these objectives, the emergence of processual devices and their prescribed function in each company will be looked at first. Then, data that describe the functioning of these devices and that provide some basis for evaluating their effectiveness will be presented. An attempt will be made to isolate some of the factors that influenced the performance of these devices in each company.

In examining the functioning of committees and similar small groups, we could focus on many aspects of their internal processes, such as role differentiation, leadership behavior, or the phases of group emotions. Here, however, our interest is in uniformities in these groups within each company, which may be related to their effectiveness as integrative devices. For this reason our focus will be on some of the uniformities that were present in all the committees or teams in each organization.

The Emergence of Processual Devices

In seeking committees and teams that would support our expectations that processual integrative devices would emerge in each company, two criteria were established. First, the committee or team would have to be cross-functional, with representatives from the basic subsystems and the linking subsystems. Second, one of its major functions would have to be to provide a setting for the integration activities related to new product innovation. By using these criteria, we are continuing to focus on interdepartmental relationships where there was a high degree of requisite integration in innovating products.

PROCESSUAL DEVICES AT RHODY AND PROCTER CHEMICALS

In the product group with which this study deals, there were two levels of integrative processual devices at R&P which met our criteria. At the upper echelon was the Business Team, made up of the group sales manager, the laboratory director from Research (who represented all research activities), the product section manager from the Production Division, and the product group manager from the Integrative subsystem. A fifth member of the team was the business manager for this group of products, who was on the staff of the Plastics Department manager. At the lower echelon were three Goal Teams, each of which focused on a certain industrial market to which the products were sold. On each Goal Team were the sales product manager for the industrial market, the Integrative unit section head for the industrial market, who was chairman, and the group leader from Research for the industrial market. The plant manager served as the Production representative on all three Goal Teams.

These devices had been formally recognized for only about a year at the time of this study, but they had existed informally over the life of the product group. This made it difficult to find an explicit formal statement of their function. Perhaps the best way to get a clear understanding of the role of these teams is to quote the business manager for this group of products as he described their formalization and their function:

> There is a general concept underlying the Business Teams and that is that we are trying to form a business. We want to break the company down into businesses. The idea of the general principle came down from above and [the Plastics Department manager] then decided to break plastics down into several businesses. We were already really working in this fashion though we weren't calling them businesses. For example, we were already organized around this product group. As far as the Business Teams were concerned, the only direction from above was to set them up and organize along business lines in these various areas. We felt we had to look at each market within the product group and for this reason we developed the Goal Teams.
>
> These teams are primarily a coordinating committee. The Goal Teams decide where they want this family of products to go in their market. The Business Team coordinates and approves the plans of these three Goal Teams.
>
> The business is a profit center and it is our responsibility to look out for the profits of this business. While we haven't yet delegated the profit responsibility to the Goal Teams, we are tending in that direction. They know if their business is profitable and which of the products is profitable. What we want the men on the Goal Teams to find out is that by sitting down together they are able to come up with a coordinated plan. Members of the Goal Teams are also in a position to take immediate action on their plans.

The manager of this product group in the Integrative unit further clarified the requisite role of these teams:

Management has told these fellows [the Goal Team], 'We want you to decide what is best for business and then you tell us how to run it. We don't want to tell you how to run it.' We assume that nobody in the company knows more about this particular group of products than the fellows on the team. We really say to them, 'You tell us how to run it.' They don't get the profit and loss statement on the Goal Teams, but they do know what products are profitable and which are not and they know the sales figures.

The initial major task of each Goal Team was to establish long-range plans for their market area. This involved not only determining the growth potential of existing markets, but also a consideration of the type of new product directions they should take. On the basis of these plans, the teams were expected to make estimates of the research, development, sales, and production efforts necessary to achieve their objectives. Having established these objectives and having gotten the approval of the Business Team, the Goal Teams were expected to coordinate efforts in the various functional areas to accomplish their objectives. One important aspect of this activity was coordinating the research, development, sales, and production of new and improved products. As we shall see shortly, team members devoted a portion of their formal meetings, as well as informal contacts, to facilitating the process of scientific transfer.

In this brief description of the prescribed function of the Business and Goal Teams, we see the emergence of integrative devices that meet both of our criteria. They were intended to integrate the activities of all the functional areas, particularly when there was a high need for integration in the development of products.

Processual Devices at the Crown Chemical Company

At Crown there were several committees and teams in existence, all of which were intended to facilitate coordination between functional areas and, to some extent, were concerned with the development of new products. At the highest level of the division was the Management Committee comprised of the general manager, assistant general manager, the marketing director, sales director, director of manufacturing, and the research director. This group was responsible for coordinating divisional policies, including the approval of the commercialization of all new products. At a lower level was the Product Management Committee; because of its pervasive role, it will be our chief concern here.

The detailed planning and integrating of activities related to scientific transfer was supposed to take place in the several Product Management Committees. These committees were also expected to deal with other matters, such as the solution of particular major customer problems. There were five committees, one for each product area. The members of each were the laboratory director responsible for research on the product group; the production department manager responsible for production of those products; and the product manager, who acted as chairman. If there was a technical representative working as an assistant to the product manager, he was also a member of the committee, serving as secretary. There was no representative from the Sales subsystem, since the product manager was expected to be knowledgeable in sales matters and to represent their interests.

A further clarification of the role of the Product Management Committee can be obtained from a memorandum written by the Research Director describing the selection and programming of research projects:

> The Division has five main product lines, each of which is headed by a product manager. He is responsible for the profitability of the line and coordinates research, production, and marketing activities. He does not have line responsibility for these functions. Each product line has a Product Management Committee made up of Research, Production, and [Integrative] representatives. The product manager is

chairman of the committee. The decision to include a project in the research program is normally made by the Product Management Committee.

Thus these committees provided the setting in which decisions to initiate projects were to be made; they also were supposed to review the progress of research projects and the commercial development of products in their segment of the product line.

Except that the Sales subsystem was not represented directly, the Product Management Committees meet both of our criteria. They provided liaison across functional areas in relation to a range of activities, but particularly in matters related to scientific transfer. In both companies, then, we have found support for our expectation that processual devices would emerge.

The Functioning of Processual Devices in Both Systems

In the balance of our discussion of processual devices, our data deal primarily with one set in each company—the Goal Teams at R&P and the Product Management Committees at Crown. The scientific transfer process requires a high degree of collaboration between functional areas, especially at their lower echelons where intimate technical and marketing knowledge is available. Therefore, because these sets of devices provide the setting in which integration at the lowest level was conducted in each company, they will serve as the basis for our study of the functioning and effectiveness of these devices. Also of interest in this respect is the manner in which their effectiveness was influenced by integration activities at higher levels in each organization.

We will first present data gathered at meetings and in interviews at both companies. Once the evidence for both systems is before us, we will then explore some of the factors that seemed to influence the performance of these devices.

THE GOAL TEAMS AT RHODY AND PROCTER

At R&P, the researcher attended meetings of the various Goal Teams, as well as of the Business Team. The data presented here are intended to provide a sense of the contents of these discussions and of the attitudes of the team members concerning their effectiveness.

An agenda (Figure V–1) for one of the meetings of a Goal Team attended by the researcher indicates several general characteristics of these meetings. First, only the four members of the

Figure V–1—Sample Agenda Goal Team— Rhody & Procter Chemicals

Members	Guests*
Integrative Unit Section Head, Chairman	Pilot Plant Engineer
Research Group Leader	Laboratory Technician, ERL
Production Plant Manager	
Sales Product Manager	

Agenda

1. Production status of [New Product]
   a. Production problems
   b. Inventory
   c. Customer reactions
2. [Another New Product]
   a. Status of work being done in ERL
3. Status of [a third New Product]
   a. Customer evaluation
4. Cost reduction project
   a. Short process time [product] (pilot plant report)
   b. Status of new product with Department of Agriculture
5. Color problem on [New Product]
   a. Analytical lab report
   b. Research lab report

* These guests remained at the meeting only long enough to deliver reports and discuss any problems connected with them.

team were present for the duration of the meeting. Individuals who had particular technical information on a special project were asked to attend the meeting for only the time necessary to discuss that particular problem. The meeting dealt almost entirely with new products or processes and other future developments. For example, even the subject of the cost reduction report (item #4) dealt with the development of a significant new process that could reduce processing time by a considerable amount. It should be noted, however, that the researcher was informed by team members that this particular meeting did not consider as many major long-term matters as some other sessions did.

As the group was assembling at this meeting the Sales Product Manager began the discussion:

> PRODUCT MANAGER: Before [the Plant Manager] gets here . . . He knows what is going on since he runs the material through the plant. . . . I thought I would tell you sales are up 29 percent for last month. . . .
>
> SECTION HEAD: Hey, that's good. . . . Do you have any more good news?
>
> GROUP LEADER: That's the way to start the day off.

The Product Manager discussed the sources of the increased sales volume as the other members took a few notes. This discussion lasted approximately five minutes as the other members of the team passed on several pieces of miscellaneous information. During a pause in the conversation, the Section Head asked if they were ready to start on the agenda items. There was general agreement that they were, so he asked the Plant Manager to introduce the first item, which involved certain production problems with a new product. The Plant Manager explained that the problem was caused by changes in external temperatures and humidity. He read data which explained how these changes seemed to influence the composition of the material. When he concluded the Section Head asked a question:

SECTION HEAD: Is this speeding up filtering?
PLANT MANAGER: Yes, because we don't have to handle as much residue.

The Plant Manager then went on to explain that part of the difficulty was also caused by the odor of the material. As he did so the Section Head and the Group Leader asked questions to clarify technical points.

GROUP LEADER: Can't you reduce the [content of certain materials]?
PLANT MANAGER: We don't know yet. What we propose to do is to add some the next time we try it.
GROUP LEADER: I don't think we can live with the level we have now.
PLANT MANAGER: I agree. We had a meeting this morning and I asked [one of the process engineers] to investigate this.
GROUP LEADER: This is something we could give to [the Pilot Plant Manager in the ERL] when he gets started again. When is he going to start running again?

There was a brief discussion about when this pilot plant, which had been out of operation for a short period, would be operating again. It was determined that it would be running within a month.

GROUP LEADER: We have to get this taken care of.
PRODUCT MANAGER: Won't [Plant Manager's] process work take care of this?
PLANT MANAGER: It should. I expect to pick up a few per cent.
GROUP LEADER: That's right. I think it should pick up a few per cent, but we still want to get a fix on the exact cause.

He and the Plant Manager discussed this problem for a few minutes and then the Group Leader said:

GROUP LEADER: The man who is working on it [in Research] thinks he knows the cause. He is running tests on it. He is convinced in his own mind about what is wrong, but he isn't certain. He isn't sure enough to present it to [the Plant Manager] because he doesn't have the facts yet.

PLANT MANAGER: Well, when you have the outcome tell us. We want to get out from under this one too.

GROUP LEADER: You know when we get the facts we will be over. But I still think [the ERL Pilot Plant] could help with some runs on this.

They all discussed whether or not the ERL Pilot Plant could help on the problem and after a brief discussion agreed that it could.

SECTION HEAD: Will you, [Group Leader], check with [the ERL Pilot Plant Manager] and see if he can work on this problem?

The Group Leader agreed to do this, and all four members made a note of the decision. They then proceeded to discuss the next item on the agenda. After a brief preliminary discussion, they were interrupted by the appearance of a Laboratory Technician from the ERL.* He was introduced to the members of the team and then began to explain his findings about certain qualities of new materials and to show samples of them. The members of the team expressed satisfaction with his work. The discussion focused upon obtaining a detailed understanding of the data.

PRODUCT MANAGER: Could you explain the test you ran and the formulations you used?

TECHNICIAN: Well, we tested for heat stability (he explained this test in detail).

PLANT MANAGER: That's heat stability, what about light?

The Section Head and the Product Manager replied simultaneously that heat was the big problem. The Plant Manager agreed that this was true, and the Technician continued to explain the heat test.

PLANT MANAGER: Is this polymerized?

TECHNICIAN: No.

* The Laboratory Technician, who was about 20 years of age, had been invited to attend the meeting as a substitute for his Group Leader who was otherwise occupied.

PLANT MANAGER: Then it is added afterward.

TECHNICIAN: Yes. It is mechanically mixed in. (He discussed the details briefly.) If that is all of your questions, I'd like to ask a few questions which would help us.

He asked several questions which each of the members of the team answered.

PRODUCT MANAGER: This test we are using is pretty tough. Some customers would let it go lower.

SECTION HEAD: Yes, but we want to run all the tests against a control, so we know what the limits are for future use.

PRODUCT MANAGER: We don't want that to preclude setting limits which are acceptable now.

PLANT MANAGER: How does [another product] compare?

PRODUCT MANAGER: Better.

PLANT MANAGER: Couldn't we use it as a control?

SECTION HEAD: I think it is better to have higher tests.

PRODUCT MANAGER: Are we missing something by having a higher test? That's really what I am asking. I don't know myself.

The Laboraory Technician interrupted and explained their rationale for wanting higher tests. He then continued with this suggestion.

TECHNICIAN: After we have tested it this way, we can very easily repeat it at lower temperatures.

SECTION HEAD: I think we would feel better if we knew it was able to stand higher temperatures. Then [the Research Group Leader] would know where we stand for the future.

PRODUCT MANAGER: I just don't want us to miss any bets by setting too high standards.

All four men discussed this calmly for several minutes. The Product Manager continued to express concern about using too tight a control, but the Group Leader and the Section Head argued for the more rigorous test. The Plant Manager agreed with the Product Manager. The Section Head then referred back to the Technician's suggestion.

SECTION HEAD: You could run these at both a higher and lower temperature. It wouldn't cost us much, would it?

TECHNICIAN: Yes, we can do it very easily.

SECTION HEAD: Why don't you do that? That way we will know the outside limits and also how it performs within present requirements.

PRODUCT MANAGER: I think that would be a good idea.

The others agreed with this resolution. The Group Leader explained some technical details to the Technician. As the Technician was preparing to leave, the Section Head summarized what they wanted done before the next meeting and the other team members nodded their agreement and made notes about the discussion.

A few moments later the Pilot Plant Engineer arrived so the group interrupted its discussion and decided to cover the topic with which he was concerned.* The engineer explained that the object of the process improvement project in the pilot plant was to make substantial reductions in process time. He also explained that the idea suggested by the Research scientists didn't work out completely in the pilot plant, and he described several modifications he had made which seemed to be working better. At several points he was interrupted by questions from the Group Leader, the Plant Manager, and the Section Head, all of whom were quite pleased with the progress he was making.

The Group Leader summarized the discussion.

GROUP LEADER: Then you have to reduce [certain specifications]. If you do that would you say we are ready for a larger run?

ENGINEER: Assuming other properties are right.

GROUP LEADER: What problems do you see, [Plant Manager]?

PLANT MANAGER: We would have to make a few minor equipment changes, but I would say it looks pretty good. (He briefly listed the necessary changes.)

GROUP LEADER: [The Engineer] is anxious to move on to other things and he feels that he has contributed all he can here and

* The pilot plant was part of the Research subsystem.

[another engineer] is ready to take it into the 200 gallon plant. But I feel he shouldn't get sidetracked until we have these other properties checked out. (To the Engineer) Is that O.K.?

ENGINEER: Yes, that is all right with me.

SECTION HEAD: Yes, I think we ought to keep him with us on this until that is worked out. How will you [Engineer] proceed on these other properties?

The Section Head, Group Leader, Plant Manager, and the Engineer discussed the next steps for several minutes until they were all certain about what was going to be done.

PLANT MANAGER: Should we begin to get equipment ready?

SECTION HEAD: I think I would hold off until he gets these other things worked out.

PLANT MANAGER: Well, I am concerned because, as I don't have to tell you, we are getting close to plant capacity and we are anxious to get started.

GROUP LEADER: I think we are a year away. (To the Engineer) What do you think?

ENGINEER: That sounds too long.

PLANT MANAGER: I'd say more like six months.

SECTION HEAD: That's more like it. We still have to check performance with the customer.

GROUP LEADER: We already slipped some in on a shipment to [a large customer] and they didn't complain.

PRODUCT MANAGER: (Laughing) Don't forget they aren't our only customer.

There was a lengthy discussion between all four team members about the costs and details of plant modifications. It was agreed that the Plant Manager would proceed to plan the details for the changes, but would wait for the larger test runs before making any modifications. The Section Head summarized by saying they would wait on equipment changes for a few months while the pilot plant work was completed, but that the Plant Manager would go ahead with planning. The Plant Manager agreed, making notes about what he was to do; and then the Section Head and the Group Leader clarified for the Engineer how much time to spend on the larger pilot plant runs. The Engineer then departed.

The Section Head next suggested that they resume the discussion they had interrupted when the Engineer arrived. This they did for several minutes, after which they agreed to move on to the next item. The Section Head explained that another Goal Team was being assigned the task of looking into a major new product. This other team dealt with another customer industry. He concluded his remarks:

SECTION HEAD: There may be some applications for us, but I doubt it because the price is too high. I don't think we need to worry about it.

The Product Manager and the Section Head discussed this for several minutes with the Product Manager taking the position that they should consider the possibilities of finding applications for this new product in their industrial area.

PRODUCT MANAGER: The customer doesn't need heat or light stability on this product. Without these properties it could be cheaper than existing material. I don't think we will know what we can do unless we really try it. We need something to attack the customer with in applications where I think this [new material] would work.

SECTION HEAD: The prospect of selling the material at $0.60 and competing with other stuff at $0.56 isn't very good.

PRODUCT MANAGER: I think it is good. We can improve performance. I think we should put pressure on [the other Goal Team] to look at our industry, assuming polymer changes.

SECTION HEAD: Assuming polymer changes, that is a different story.

For several minutes, the Section Head and the Product Manager continued to discuss the question of a correct appraisal of the market for this product. The discussion never became heated, although both men stuck to their positions. The Product Manager concluded this phase of the discussion.

PRODUCT MANAGER: I think we deserve to have them work on it for us. I think otherwise it will be just used for [other applications].

SECTION HEAD: Assuming the price comes down eventually.

PRODUCT MANAGER: That will be too late. I think we have to come to an understanding with this new team now.

SECTION HEAD: I would agree with you, except for [a competitor's product].

PRODUCT MANAGER: We can't let that chase us out. You can see what has happened to [a declining industrial market]. We have to protect our business.

GROUP LEADER: I think we should take a look at this. It can't do us any harm. Could we have [another Section Head] come talk to us at the next meeting? They are the ones who have this stuff and we can see how they feel about reducing costs.

SECTION HEAD: We could do that.

He and the Group Leader discussed this approach for several minutes and the Product Manager again stressed his position.

PRODUCT MANAGER: I think we have to have somebody work on this. We need some effort.

GROUP LEADER: I think we should let them come in and have their say so.

PRODUCT MANAGER: I agree. If there is any loophole, price reductions, and so on, I think we should find out about it and get them going because it could be an ideal situation for us. The plant will be located in the same area as our biggest customers.

SECTION HEAD: O.K. Let's get [another Section Head] in here next time, to see what they can do. I'll see that he gets over here to discuss it. I guess we should find out about it.

The team then turned to the next item on the agenda. This dealt with a new application for a product which held out considerable promise of a high sales volume. The Section Head and the Group Leader had just returned from an industry trade show, where they had met with the potential major customer; they reviewed their discussions especially for the benefit of the Plant Manager, so that he would have as much information as possible for scheduling future production. There was considerable confusion about the customer's intention. One reason for this was that a member of the Business Team had also been at the trade show. This executive, having talked to the customer and feeling that an order was imminent, had wired the Plant Manager from the trade show and told him to plan time in his schedule. The team members had been quite concerned with this interference in their prerogatives, and the Section Head informed the other members how he had resolved the problem.

> SECTION HEAD: I talked to [the executive involved] and told him that we had agreed that [the Group Leader] would maintain liaison between us and the customer on this project. He apologized for getting involved. I am certain he will stay out of it now. So you [Plant Manager] don't have to worry about scheduling this stuff unless [the Group Leader] indicates that it is necessary. We can get together and discuss it then.
> PLANT MANAGER: That is the way it has to be, otherwise we don't know what to expect next.
> PRODUCT MANAGER: You can't blame [the executive involved] too much. You know how it gets when you are at these shows talking to customers. They can get you all excited, if you don't have all the background information.
> GROUP LEADER: I don't know what else I can tell you [Plant Manager]. I guess I can say this; I am not as optimistic as I was before we went to the show.
> SECTION HEAD: So we just have to wait and see how the customer jumps, but [the Group Leader] is our official contact with the customer on this thing. [The other executive] doesn't count on this one. He'll stay out of it and we'll keep you [the Plant Manager] informed.

Several aspects of these meetings are evident from these excerpts. The content of the meeting focused almost exclusively upon the solution of problems related to new and developing products. There was a tendency for members of the team to persevere in their discussion of a problem until a solution was reached. When there was a disagreement between them, they did not dodge it but kept discussing the issues until a resolution was achieved. In spite of this tendency, the discussion did not seem to reach a high emotional level. The team members, in this manner, reached decisions at their own level. When a higher executive became involved in their activities, they took the initiative in remedying the situation. It is worth noting that in solving this and other problems the Integrative Section Head often played a central role. Finally, when team members needed more detailed technical information about a project for which they were responsible, they relied on the people at the operating level to provide it. With this firsthand view of the conduct of a typical meeting, we can now examine this integrative device in more general terms through the eyes of its members and other personnel at R&P.

Perhaps the most frequent point made about the functioning of the team was that they were really a formalization of methods of operating which had existed for many years. The comment of a section head in the Integrative unit emphasizes this point:

> I would say that the practice of the teams really preceded the fact. We used to have a lot of close coordination on the basis of certain unique personalities. This always existed between units. The teams just formalize what was going on.

Another fact stressed by members of the team was that they actually did make decisions that influenced profits. A product manager in Sales stated it this way:

> The teams have allowed us, as individuals, to more formally play a role in decision making, which we didn't do before. Now with the team concept we can make a decision which will affect the profit. We can see the results of our efforts more realistically than we could before. Of course, we all recognize that there are three other guys depending on our effort, so we make an effort to produce.

Not only does this product manager find himself involved in making decisions, but he also feels an obligation to carry out these decisions because others on the team are depending on his efforts.

Members of the teams sometimes had to exert considerable emotional and intellectual effort to reach a resolution of differences among them. Almost everyone interviewed mentioned this process of conflict resolution. A section head in the Integrative subsystem spoke about resolving these differences without relying on higher management:

> We try to resolve things within our area of responsibility. Sometimes this is very difficult. Sometimes what we are doing is hazy. If we feel we might be going outside our area we advise the Business Team what we have done. They usually have to go along because we have already done it. Once recently they called us in and asked us why we had done something and after we had explained it they agreed it was the right thing to have done. We could use this mechanism to buck it up to the Business Team, but I think this would be a weak committee and a weak individual and I am not willing to give my freedom up. They give you all the rope you need. If you need their help they are there, if you don't need them, don't bother them. If I am going to make a broad decision affecting our policy in the industry, I will ask for help, if I am still doubtful about what to do. If it is a major decision, it is foolish not to let the Business Team kick it around first. The Goal Team might not know all the implications for R&P.

A product manager indicated how these things were resolved in the Goal Teams, stressing particularly the concern of members with the realities of getting their task done, as opposed to satisfying management's criteria:

> Our problems get thrashed out in committee. We work them over until everybody agrees this is the best effort you can make. We may decide this isn't good enough, then we may decide to ask for more people, more plant, and so forth. We all sometimes have to take a modification and be realistic and say this is the best we can do.
>
> In recent meetings we have had a thrashing around about manpower needs. At first we didn't have much agreement, but we kept thrashing around and finally agreed on what was the best we could do. We didn't let the percentages from last year guide us. First, we decided what we wanted to do, and then we decided what it was going to take to do what we wanted. At first we tried to block it out by the traditional guide lines, but it didn't work because we couldn't

get close to what we wanted. It took a while to realize this. Then we said, 'to hell with the Business Team, let's tell them what we really think is necessary. It is going to cost us this much money for what we want to do. It is up to them to decide whether they think we are asking for too much or if it is good. But we are on record as saying this is what should be done.' When we advance proposals like this, we give them something to think about. If you follow the guide lines, you are just spending the money for the sake of spending it.

Another product manager also stressed the difficulties in resolving these issues, but indicated that he felt committed to the team's decision, even when he disagreed:

I may want to do some work on a polymer; the [Integrative] guy may say, 'Let's get the customer to change his process instead.' A Research guy may say we need both. It is the way we do it that becomes argumentative and rightfully so. These things take several meetings to work out, but we are never really stalemated. We have decided in our committee that we won't stalemate. There is more than one way to our ends. If I don't agree with the others, then I abdicate my position. Sometimes gracefully and sometimes not. We had a disagreement about releasing confidential information to a customer and had quite a discussion about it. This was only the second time we had gotten so formal as to have a vote. I was outvoted three to one, but that afternoon I was the one who had to call the customer and give him the information as we had decided.

From these comments we see that conflict was resolved by confronting the issues until a workable solution was reached. We also have found that the members of the team were committed to these decisions even though they might not agree with them. Finally members of the Goal Team tended to view the superordinate Business Team as a body that had broader knowledge of company policy and that was available for consultation on wider matters but not for resolving disputes within the team. Let us now turn to some comments from personnel at R&P which indicate their impressions of the effectiveness of the teams as integrative devices.

A section head in the Integrative subsystem expressed a view that was typical of those of others in the Department:

> Since we have had the Goal Teams, we are working more closely with other groups. It is really working out. In the past, Production was reticent to give us information and they wanted to keep the prerogative of making process changes. Since this team concept, there has been a greater understanding and a greater exchange of information. I feel closer to the Research and Production departments because of this. We always have felt close to Sales.

He went on to indicate that the present set of teams had some unique features which had not always been present in other such devices; this is a point which will take on more significance when we begin to compare R&P and Crown:

> The Goal Teams are not the first committees we have had at this level. Years back when I worked on other products we had other Goal Teams. This was many years ago. We had 10 to 15 people at these meetings and they were from all ranks. My feeling at that time was you were just outranked. The area that wanted the most pressure would bring in the most rank and this was where the activity went. It's better to have people of equal rank working together. The superiors haven't sat in on any of the Goal Teams so far.

The Plant Manager also felt that the teams had been useful in improving relationships between departments:

> I would say right now the relations between all the groups are better than they have ever been before and I would say our cooperation is better. There were many years when Sales and [the Integrative unit] unilaterally told Production what to do. Now I feel that Production has a stronger voice than ever before. I don't know what has brought this about. The committees may have had something to do with it—just bringing people together can create a team spirit. I would say that the teams have also produced a much better flow of information. It has brought research people out of their pure research activity and into a broader understanding of the business.

The members of the Sales subsystem also felt the teams were facilitating their relationship with other units: a sales product manager expressed this view:

The teams take a lot of time. I used to have eight hours to my-self and I thought I could get a lot more done. I feel now that I spend time on committees instead of making autocratic decisions, but this really isn't a disadvantage because we are getting better decisions. It affords me something I have never had before. I have never had a great deal of contact with research. I know, in the past, information was fed back to research and occasionally misinterpreted. I don't think we will have that problem now. I don't care how [the Plant Manager] runs his plant, but if he tells me something is difficult for him, I try to steer the customers away from it. I think he sees our problems too. This could have all been done before but I would have had to go out of my way to get to know [the Plant Manager]. This would have probably taken more time than with the committees.

The group leaders in Research, who were also on the teams, indicated a similar satisfaction with their performance. One stated it this way:

The Goal Teams as we now have them are a great improvement. It gets us together so the problems can be talked out and projects sifted out. In this way we are pretty sure we are working on worth-while projects. One functional group can't go off alone. We are all aware that we are dependent on each other. If one member balks then we are all in trouble. It makes you sit down and agree on what your goals are. Once we have put these things down on paper we as a group are committed to them. I would say the most important man at these meetings is the guy from [the Integrative unit]. He is the chairman of the team. He is the most centrally located guy, and he is the coordinator.

I would say the good thing about the Goal Teams is that you can begin to see farther ahead. When I was in research, I used to think of the process as sort of a hill, and I couldn't see over the top beyond [the Integrative unit]. But now you can see the sales hill and the production hill and it broadens your little world.

One factor of particular interest is the coordinating role played by the Integrative representative. As indicated in the last chapter, the intermediate position of this subsystem in occupational orien-tation and structure facilitated this linking role. Its importance to the functioning of the teams is also indicated by the following remark made by another group leader in Research:

> One good thing on the team is that [the Integrative unit] is close enough to Sales to know what they are doing and close enough to Research to know what we are doing. I think this is why they made the [Integrative] men chairmen.

We can draw several conclusions about the processual integrative device at R&P. Personnel considered it to be an effective linking device. It provided a setting in which members, without relying on their superiors, made decisions by confronting and, usually, resolving their differences. Members generally showed a high level of commitment to decisions made. Finally, the teams had in the Integrative member one individual with a more balanced view of the problems confronting them. After examining the Product Management Committees at Crown, we will return to a more detailed analysis of those factors that seem to account for the effectiveness of the Goal Teams.

THE PRODUCT MANAGEMENT COMMITTEES AT THE CROWN CHEMICAL COMPANY

The researcher attended meetings of different Product Management Committees at Crown. A typical agenda for one of these meetings is presented in Figure V–2. One generalization we can make from it is that, although there were only four members formally on the committee, the actual number of participants present for the entire meeting was usually double this number and often more. A second characteristic of all the meetings was that a large portion of the meeting was devoted to the review of sales reports and inventory levels and a general exchange of information about these and related matters, especially as these dealt with newly commercialized products.

A typical meeting was attended by those personnel listed in Figure V–2. After the Product Manager had spent a half hour comparing actual sales with budgeted figures, he was interrupted by his superior, the Department Manager, who asked a question

**Figure V–2—Sample Agenda, Product Management Committee—
Crown Chemical Company**

Members	Guests*
Product Manager, Chairman	Process Engineer$_1$
Technical Representative, Secretary	Process Engineer$_2$
Production Department Manager	Research Group Leader$_1$
Laboratory Director	Research Group Leader$_2$
	Research Group Leader$_3$
	Integrative Department Manager
	Quality Control Manager

Agenda

1. Approval of minutes
2. Review of actual sales versus budget
3. Product delivery schedules and inventory status
4. Review of plant problems (6 items)
5. Review of sales problems (1 item)
6. Review of research problems and new products (5 items)
7. Future research program
8. Other business

* These guests remained throughout the meeting.

about a new addition to the plant. One of the Process Engineers replied:

PROCESS ENGINEER: We will be building inventory from the time it comes on stream until May. I should think that by that time we will have enough inventory to begin shipping.

LABORATORY DIRECTOR: How much behind schedule will that make us?

PROCESS ENGINEER: The contractor thinks he will be out by the first of the month and that should make us about a month later than we expected.

This statement was challenged by one of the Group Leaders, but after some clarification by the Engineer there was general agreement that the building program was just one month behind schedule.

PRODUCTION DEPARTMENT MANAGER: While we are on the subject of the new plant I want to make one point. I don't want to let our present schedule at [the old plant] guide us in the new one. My bosses and I are under considerable pressure to keep the work week within union contract limits. I don't think we can do that and meet the present schedule. We will have to be able to arrange the new schedule accordingly. We want to put ourselves in the position where we are running the plant, not the union.

PRODUCT MANAGER: That's good to hear.

PRODUCTION DEPARTMENT MANAGER: That is the way it is going to be.

PRODUCT MANAGER: Well it is good to know that; but I don't think it should create any problems for us.

The meeting then returned to a discussion of current inventory levels with the Production Department Manager reading the figures for 20 minutes while the others listened. He then reported on the progress he had made in processing a particular new product.

PRODUCTION DEPARTMENT MANAGER: We seem to have the process under good control. I would say that most of the problems we have had, have been taken care of, so I really don't have much to say about it this month. Things look good.

LABORATORY DIRECTOR: Will the costs be different than we thought?

PRODUCTION DEPARTMENT MANAGER: They are slightly higher now, but we have learned a number of things which will enable us to get this under control.

GROUP LEADER: Do you have good operating procedures on it?

PRODUCTION DEPARTMENT MANAGER: Yes, I think so.

The discussion continued to focus on an exchange of information about several other processing problems, with agreement that Research would examine one problem for Production. The Product Manager then introduced the subject of sales problems:

PRODUCT MANAGER: The next thing on the agenda is the sales problems. We have a sales problem on [one new product]. Most of you have read [Group Leader₂'s] report from his trip to Chicago and Cleveland. He has come up with conclusions which I agree with. The product does lack hardness.

The Product Manager read several paragraphs of the report which indicated that customers found the product to be insufficiently hard. He then turned to the Integrative Department Manager, suggesting that he might want to say something:

> INTEGRATIVE DEPARTMENT MANAGER: I do want to say something, but I don't know if now is the proper time. There is no doubt that we have a problem with this one.
> LABORATORY DIRECTOR: I don't think it is a research problem. We have done as much about this as we can.
> INTEGRATIVE DEPARTMENT MANAGER: We do have a problem, whether it is research or sales. We will have to get the customer trained to use it, or else correct it ourselves.
> TECHNICAL REPRESENATIVE: (To Laboratory Director) Do you have any ideas on the hardness problem?
> LABORATORY DIRECTOR: We've got ideas, but we have to test them on the customer's equipment.
> PRODUCT MANAGER: We can run it at the customer's any time.

The Integrative Department Manager and the Laboratory Director then spent several minutes discussing the problem. The Product Manager mentioned that a second big customer was interested in having some of the product to test, but that a large batch couldn't be shipped until two months later. The Laboratory Director then mentioned that in any case it would be necessary for this particular customer to use an additive.

> LABORATORY DIRECTOR: The customer is going to have to use [the additive] if he wants a mark-proof surface.
> PRODUCT MANAGER: I agree with you, but the trouble is that how hard it is doesn't depend on our customer, but on the end user. It is the coater who is putting it on the material. How can you get him to do it?
> LABORATORY DIRECTOR: We aren't marketing it right. We have to put pressure on the coater to use it right. If [a competitor] is doing it, our customers can.
> PRODUCT MANAGER: I am glad you picked that one, because it just so happens they aren't doing it that way.

The Integrative Department Manager entered the discussion. He, a Group Leader, and the Laboratory Director discussed it for several minutes, until he concluded:

INTEGRATIVE DEPARTMENT MANAGER: Well, if we can't make the material until later, we can't do anything about it now anyway.

GROUP LEADER: That's true.

LABORATORY DIRECTOR: We still have to go to the coaters and show them how to do it. We can tell them other people are using it, and show them how.

INTEGRATIVE DEPARTMENT MANAGER: Then we are directing them to a particular formulation.

PRODUCT MANAGER: You [the Laboratory Director] are barking up the wrong tree.

This discussion continued and became increasingly heated. The Laboratory Director finally suggested that the product be tested by another large customer. The Product Manager objected:

PRODUCT MANAGER: They are just too busy to look at it.

LABORATORY DIRECTOR: We will send somebody to help them.

PRODUCT MANAGER: You know something [Laboratory Director]? We offered to do this. But just to satisfy you we will try to go back and get them to look at it.

LABORATORY DIRECTOR: I still think we should get to the end user and get them to put pressure on our customers.

INTEGRATIVE DEPARTMENT MANAGER: We will spend money on advertising to them when your tests prove out. I just want to make sure we don't drop the ball.

LABORATORY DIRECTOR: We won't drop the ball, but I do think we should get out and give them an incentive to try it. We are so close in hardness I can't believe that we can't get them to use it. It is just a matter of better formulation.

PRODUCT MANAGER: If you think it is so simple, why don't you figure it out in the lab and tell them how?

INTEGRATIVE DEPARTMENT MANAGER: I think we have dwelled on this long enough.

LABORATORY DIRECTOR: I think so too.

The Product Manager moved to the next item on the agenda.

Several important facts about the Product Management Committees stand out from these excerpts. First, a large portion of the meeting was devoted to an exchange of information about current inventory and sales problems. Second, when conflict developed in the meeting, there was a tendency to avoid it and move on to the next matter without resolving it. Finally, the senior executives who attended the meeting as guests, often became centrally involved in the discussion.

Similar characteristics of this processual device can be noticed from excerpts of a meeting of a second Product Management Committee. The participants included the four formal members and a Product Manager, Technical Representative, Production Department Manager, and Laboratory Director. Also in attendance were the Plant Operations Manager (the superior of the Production Department Manager), a Quality Control Representative, and three Group Leaders from the Laboratory.

The first hour of this meeting was spent exchanging information about sales trends and inventory levels. At the end of this period, the Production Department Manager read a report on quality control improvements which initiated a discussion between the Product Manager, the Technical Representative and the Quality Control Manager about the product discoloring under certain conditions. The Product Manager finally ended the discussion by referring to minutes of a past meeting and asking several questions about changes in production procedures, which had created a problem of plasticity in a new product.

> PRODUCT MANAGER: [Group Leader$_1$] and [a Process Engineer] established in a meeting in [the Plant Manager's] office that the plasticity was too low.
> QUALITY CONTROL MANAGER: Yeah, when?

Group Leader$_1$ explained what the agreement was and the Laboratory Director nodded his agreement. The Product Manager agreed and began to ask a question, when the Plant Operations Manager interrupted:

> OPERATIONS MANAGER: We made it work for product 621 for [a customer].
> PRODUCT MANAGER: What will we do if we can't make it work for others? We will have to change the 'specs,' won't we?
> PRODUCTION DEPARTMENT MANAGER: Then the question becomes, with new 'specs,' how do we make it?

PRODUCT MANAGER: Look at it this way, we can't sell it unless we can make it in lower 'specs.'

PRODUCTION DEPARTMENT MANAGER: I agree but someone keeps scheduling it with the old 'specs.'

The Product Manager and the Production Department Manager argued for several minutes about whether the specifications had been changed. The Quality Control Manager interrupted them, contending that he had sent Group Leader₁ a letter about it.

GROUP LEADER₁: No, I don't have a letter. I didn't get any letter yet.

QUALITY CONTROL MANAGER: Then I will read it.

He began to read a lengthy letter which he had written explaining the problem of plasticity. He was interrupted by a question from Group Leader₁, who was visibly angry. The Quality Control Manager replied:

QUALITY CONTROL MANAGER: I'll get to that, but I'll explain what we have been doing first.

He then explained the various tests which he had performed and read a list of figures which indicated that the plasticity was acceptable when the product left the plant. The Laboratory Director interrupted him with a whistle and asked to have the figures re-read. After the Quality Control Manager had done so, he said:

QUALITY CONTROL MANAGER: Is this what we are talking about?

GROUP LEADER₁: Let me say something here. (To the Quality Control Manager) Those figures you read don't cover the whole thing. You didn't mention the other 20 tons, which were shipped.

QUALITY CONTROL MANAGER: That is up to you.

GROUP LEADER₁: You are leaving a hell of a lot out.

The Quality Control Manager and Group Leader₁ then raised their voices as they discussed whether the figures being discussed were 'official,' or whether they should use statistics from tests made after the material reached the customer. The Production Department Manager joined the argument on the side of the Quality Control Manager. The discussion became increasingly heated as Group Leader$_2$ became involved. At this point, the Product Manager went to a blackboard and began writing figures down from a sheet he had in front of him. (This data had come from tests performed at the customer's plant and indicated Crown material did not perform as well as a competitor's.) While he was doing this, the argument continued with the Production personnel contending their figures told the entire story, and the Research people equally certain that they did not. The Production Department Manager noticed the figures on the blackboard and told the Product Manager that they were not correct, so the Product Manager also put the Production statistics on the board.

> PRODUCTION DEPARTMENT MANAGER: Nobody is arguing that the figures aren't different. What we are saying is that it all left the plant in good condition, so maybe something happened before the customer used it.
> PRODUCT MANAGER: I don't care where it happened. We have to keep the plasticity low. It is up to Production and Research to solve it.
> QUALITY CONTROL MANAGER: How do we know ours isn't older than the competitor's.
> PRODUCT MANAGER: I checked it. The competitor's is actually older than ours.
> QUALITY CONTROL MANAGER: Then we do have a problem.

Group Leader$_3$ entered the discussion for the first time indicating that there had been recent process changes which might have affected the product. Production personnel discussed among themselves whether this had influenced the material in question. Finally the Operations Manager asked the Product Manager:

> OPERATIONS MANAGER: What are your plans?
> PRODUCT MANAGER: This is a problem I want Research and Production to get together on and work out.
> OPERATIONS MANAGER: That isn't what I mean. Are you going to test it?

The Product Manager explained his plan for testing the material, but ended his remarks by saying, 'I still want Research and Production to get together and work this out.' He then turned to the Laboratory Director who had stayed out of the previous discussion saying:

> PRODUCT MANAGER: Well, [Laboratory Director], what are we going to do about the plasticity? You have been awful quiet.
> LABORATORY DIRECTOR: Well, we don't know what's wrong and neither does anybody else, so I'm going to talk about [another technical problem].

The Laboratory Director and the Group Leaders explained their activities in relation to this problem with another new product, but within a few minutes another argument had erupted. This continued for several minutes with both the Research and Production personnel becoming increasingly vehement. The Product Manager interrupted:

> PRODUCT MANAGER: Every week we are getting involved in these differences between Production and Research. You two have to decide these things yourselves. It is up to the top management of Research and Production to work these out, if you can't. You should meet outside and settle these things. This takes too much of the salespeople's time and we can't waste our time on these matters. It is up to you to settle it.
> OPERATIONS MANAGER: (laughing) We want to cut down on the number of meetings.
> TECHNICAL REPRESENTATIVE: This is the first dispute we have had in the last few months.
> PRODUCT MANAGER: We should never have them. Now one thing we should get down in the minutes is that Research and Production must solve these problems before this product is commercially acceptable.

Several facts stand out from these excerpts. First, the initial controversy was left unresolved and the group went on to the second problem. When a second dispute erupted, the Product Manager wanted it resolved outside the meeting. Failing this, he saw it as the duty of top management in Production and Research to resolve it. Finally, we should note that the Product Manager tended to think of himself as representing sales and for this reason didn't want to spend time resolving these technical matters.

We can obtain a further impression of the usefulness and the characteristics of the Product Management Committees by examining comments of Crown personnel gathered in interviews. A typical description of the nature of the meetings was provided by a research group leader, who attended meetings regularly:

> Unfortunately the Product Management Committees are not as much a decision-making group as I would like. Generally there is a reporting session. We don't have time going over all these things to make some of the decisions which need to be made. I would like to see more hashing out of the problems and making of decisions. Of course we do make decisions every day among us.

Many personnel saw the primary usefulness of the meetings as a setting in which information could be exchanged, but certain decisions were reached. The participants were questioned about how these decisions were made, especially when there were differences of opinion. One product manager described his actions in resolving conflicts:

> If I want something very badly and I am confronted by a roadblock, I go to top management to get the decision made. If the research managers are willing to go ahead there is no problem. If there is a conflict, then I would go to [the research director].

After explaining several problems which had occurred in a recent meeting, a group leader from Research explained how they were resolved:

> One of the controversies I mentioned was resolved by compromise. This was decided by [the research director]. I think he also made the decision in the other matter I mentioned.

A research manager also indicated that decisions were usually made by higher levels of management.

> With the [Integrative] people we can sit down and talk out problems. These problems aren't of the same magnitude as those with production. The production difficulties get worked out by [the Research Director], or [the Assistant General Manager], and [the plant Manager], or [the Division Director of Production] getting together. We had instances of this when we were trying to run a plant trial on a new product. It usually requires [the Research Director's] intercession with [the Plant Manager] or [the Division Director of Production] to get these things done.

Crown personnel were also asked to evaluate the utility of these meetings. Most personnel found that the meetings were useful as a means of keeping various personnel aware of the relevant information; however, they found several shortcomings. An Integrative department manager provided a typical comment:

> The meetings do serve the purpose for which they are intended. We do get a lot of information. I have been thinking, however, about smaller groups, where you could talk more about individual effort. At present there are always seven or eight people present, including guests, technical engineers, and sales trainees. With a smaller group it would be better. In the present group there are too many people present and we spend too much time on technical details. We should have another group to look at long-range problems, such as sales organization, or to see that we have the right people to sell the product, or that we are competitive from a sales standpoint. All these long-range problems don't get considered in our present meetings and I think it is because they are too big.

A group leader in Research expressed a similar opinion:

> The meetings get too big, so that it is impossible to discuss some important detail. A clear idea of the situation is seldom obtained. It ends up with individuals agreeing to look at different aspects of the problems. If we could make the final decision as we go on, it would be better. It would be best to have the higher echelons worry about general policy problems, while we work at the details.

A production department manager expressed the view that the meetings never resolved any of his difficulties:

I think these meetings only intensify the arguments. I haven't learned much that I didn't know already before I got to the meeting. The meeting is supposedly not to consider details, but we have no way to get to the details. It used to be that we had some knock-down drag-out fights, but then we would get things settled. But this doesn't take place any more, so now there isn't any place for us to resolve our difficulties.

These and similar comments indicate that Crown personnel found that the meetings had a limited utility for several reasons. First, they felt that the meetings tended to be too large. Second, they felt the meetings dwelled largely on the exchange of information about current problems and not enough with the solution of these or long-range problems. They felt that few problems got resolved at the meetings. These problems were either resolved outside the meetings or by higher management.

Comparison of Processual Integrative Devices

The purpose of this comparison is to attempt to understand some of the factors underlying the differences in effectiveness between the processual devices in the two systems. At Crown, members of the Product Management Committees considered them to have only a limited effectiveness; at R&P, members felt the Goal Teams were quite effective in achieving integration. Personnel in both companies tended to view these processual devices as being effective to the extent that they were helpful in resolving inter-departmental conflict and in obtaining commitment of all the members to a unified effort. The data indicate that norms had evolved within each company about appropriate behavior within these committees and teams. These norms seem to have been related to the differing degrees of effectiveness between the processual devices in the two companies.

If we were to ask the members of one of the Goal Teams at

R&P about the norms under which their team operated, we might get the following answers:

1. Attendance at our meetings should, as often as is practical, be limited to the four members.

2. We should feel responsible for profits in our market area.

3. We should use the meetings to solve problems and not just to pass information back and forth.

4. When conflicts arise, we should argue them out at the meetings ourselves, even if this takes considerable effort.

5. We should not involve our bosses in our problems.

6. We, each, should be committed to the decisions we reach as a group.

If we were to ask the same question at Crown, we could expect answers such as these:

1. We should include our superiors and subordinates as participants in our meetings.

2. We should use the meetings primarily to exchange information, but should also try to solve problems.

3. If we have difficulty in solving a problem and get into an argument, we should drop the problem.

4. If this problem is important enough to require a solution, we will ask our bosses to help solve it.

Those norms that seem to be most centrally related to the effectiveness of the processual devices are what we shall term the *norms of conflict resolution.* These are of two related types: norms about the locus of conflict resolution, and norms about the mode of conflict resolution.

The norms of conflict resolution at R&P indicated that the mode of resolution should be that of confronting differences and working them through. The locus at which this should occur was among the members of the Goal Teams. At Crown, the management level at which conflicts were expected to be resolved always seemed to be higher than at R&P. The norms concerning the mode of conflict resolution sanctioned withdrawal from disputed issues in the meetings and reliance on a higher management level to resolve conflict. Thus, the norms about the mode of conflict resolution were, as would be expected, closely related to the locus of resolution.

Both norms also appear to have been related to the complaints about the large size of the meetings at Crown. We have already noted that the uncertainty in the market and technical environment made it possible for only persons at the lower levels of management to have the detailed knowledge required for decisions. Since at Crown some of the representatives on the committees were one or two levels above the persons with intimate knowledge, it was necessary for them to bring their subordinates to the meetings. Similarly, since it was expected that the representative's superiors from the Production and Integrative departments should be involved in decisions, these individuals also attended the meetings and further swelled their size. In contrast, the members of the Goal Teams at R&P usually had both the detailed knowledge required and the sanctions necessary to make decisions. When they did not have the technical knowledge, they brought in technical "experts" to deal with each specific problem.

Examining the norms of conflict resolution also enables us to gain some understanding of the tendency of the Product Management Committees at Crown to serve largely as a forum for information exchange. Part of this may have been attributable to the sheer size of the meetings, but beyond this the norms of conflict resolution indicated problems could and should be resolved by the superiors of the committee members. The Product Management Committee was not an entirely appropriate setting in which to resolve conflict, so it was utilized as a setting in which to exchange information without necessarily expecting to reach decisions. In contrast, the norms of conflict resolution at R&P appeared to make the Goal Teams a legitimate setting in which to resolve conflict. Norms of conflict resolution, consistent with the use of the teams, existed before the teams themselves were formally recognized, and these ground rules enabled the members of the teams to work effectively together.

Finally, we should make some reference to the differences in commitment which seemed to exist between the two sets of devices. While we have very limited data about the commitment of members to decisions taken in these settings, it does seem that the degree of commitment was related to the norms of conflict resolution. At R&P, where members of the Goal Team confronted their conflicts and worked as a group at resolving them, the data seem to indicate that members were committed to act on decisions reached. At Crown, where there was a tendency to withdraw from conflict and have it resolved at higher echelons, members did not appear to be as committed to carrying out decisions. Since the team members at R&P were making the decisions themselves, they seemed to have been more identified with them. This, perhaps, was also related to the Goal Teams feeling jointly responsible for profits in their market area. This provided the teams with a clear objective which the committees at Crown did not seem to have. Having this shared goal, the teams at R&P found themselves in a position to be rewarded not only for their performance as representatives of differentiated subsystems, but also as members of groups whose task was to obtain a unified effort.

We have already referred to another difference between these two sets of processual devices which seems to be related to their effectiveness. At R&P the teams had in the Integrative representative a person who worked in a subsystem with a structure and occupational orientation that was intermediate between those of the basic subsystems. Our data indicate that in the setting of the Goal Teams this intermediate position facilitated the linking role of the Integrative representative. At Crown the Integrative subsystem was not as well placed in structure or in occupational orientation. The data about the Product Management Committee substantiated this, since the product managers seemed to be highly concerned with market matters of an immediate nature. They conceived of themselves as the 'sales' representatives on the committees. This seemed to reduce their effectiveness as integrators in the committee setting.

In summary, we have found that there were at least two factors which seemed to account for the more effective performance of the Goal Teams at R&P as compared to that of the Committees at Crown. First, we have found that the norms of conflict resolution at R&P, which emphasized resolution of conflict by confrontation within the Goal Teams, were related to the effectiveness of these integrative devices as perceived by the individuals involved. Second, the Integrative unit representative at R&P played a coordinative role on the teams.

These same factors seem to have been related to the shortcomings Crown personnel found with the Product Management Committees. The Integrative unit representative had difficulty in playing a linking role, since this subsystem was not intermediate in structure and occupational orientation. In addition, the norms of conflict resolution at Crown, which supported resolution at a level above the committee members and withdrawal from conflict in the committees, seemed to have been related to the ineffectiveness of the Product Management Committees as an integrative device.

In concluding this discussion, we should emphasize that our findings about norms of conflict resolution are highly tentative. The data indicate that the norms of conflict resolution were one important factor in the effectiveness of these committees, but no final conclusions can be drawn from them within the limits of this study. This must await a more systematic attempt to measure the differences in these norms between various organizations.

VI

Differentiation and Integration in the Two Organizational Systems

In the preceding three chapters we have conceptually dissected both organizations by first looking at the differentiation between the basic subsystems and then at the placement of the structural integrative devices and the functioning of the processual integrative devices. We now can examine the relationship between the degree of differentiation in subsystem structure and occupational orientation and the effectiveness of integration in both systems.

We have expected to find a relationship between the degree of differentiation of pairs of subsystems within one company and the difficulty in integrating their activities:

> Within any organizational system the greater the differentiation between any two subsystems in relation to the requisite integration, the greater will be the difficulties in obtaining effective integration between them.

Ideally, we would have preferred to measure the effectiveness of integration between any pair of subsystems by looking at the consequences of this relationship in terms of their joint performance in accomplishing scientific transfer. Operationally, however, it is difficult, if not impossible, to isolate this type of result for any pair of units. Instead, our measure will be the perceptions of the organization members about the effectiveness of integration between each pair of subsystems within their company.

We have also expected to find system performance related to the effectiveness of integration within each system, which in turn is related to the degree of differentiation within that system:

> If other system characteristics are similar, the greater the degree of total differentiation within each system, the greater the problems of integration and the greater the dysfunctional consequences in system performance.

One of our objectives in this study was to explore some of the system characteristics which facilitated or impaired integration; and, as we examine our data for support of this second hypothesis, the two systems will be compared to see to what extent other characteristics were similar. Some differences between systems have been pointed to in our earlier discussion, but we now will have an opportunity to examine them more closely.

In presenting support for these two hypotheses, we will continue to focus on those pairs of subsystems that have a high degree of requisite integration because of the scientific transfer process, and that require approximately the same degree of integration.

Subsystem Differentiation and Integration in the Two Systems

It may be helpful to briefly summarize the methods outlined in the Methodological Appendix for measuring differentiation between subsystems and the effectiveness of subsystem integration. In measuring the degree of differentiation between unit pairs, we divided the range of differentiation for each variable (subsystem structure and the three elements of occupational orientation) into four classes. This range included all unit pairs in both systems, so that they could not only be compared within one system, but also between systems. These classes were scored from one to four, ranging from the lowest degree of differentiation in each variable to the highest. The scores for all variables have been added to give a total differentiation score for each pair of subsystems.

To measure members' perceptions of the effectiveness of integration between subsystem pairs, we asked them to evaluate on a seven-point scale (Perceived Integration Score) the unity of effort each pair was achieving. Although this method has enabled us to make distinctions between subsystem pairs in each system and between systems, it has one shortcoming. There was a tendency in both companies for respondents to use only the upper half of the scale. This presented us with a dilemma at Crown because our clinical data indicated that members were generally more dissatisfied with the state of these relationships than the absolute scores in the questionnaires indicated. For this reason, we shall not place much confidence in the absolute values of these scores. However, by examining their relative values and the clinical data, we should be able to compare meaningfully the members' perceptions of the degree of integration being obtained.

AT RHODY AND PROCTER CHEMICALS

With the exception of the ERL, this discussion will include all those pairs of units which our earlier discussion indicated had a high degree of requisite integration: the Sales-Research relationships and the Production-Research relationships, as well as those involving the Integrative subsystem. The Sales-ERL relationship has been excluded from this discussion because, from the point of view of the majority of the respondents at R&P, the coordination activities of the Integrative subsystem obviated the need for direct collaboration between the ERL and Sales.

The data at R&P indicate that there was a relationship be-

Figure VI–1—Differentiation and Integration*—Rhody & Procter Chemicals

Subsystem Pair	Task Orientation Differentiation	Time Orientation Differentiation	Interpersonal Orientation Differentiation	Structural Differentiation	Total Differentiation Score	Perceived Integration Score
Integrative-Sales	1	1	1	2	5	1.91
Integrative-Research	1	1	1	3	6	1.97
Production-Research	3	1	3	2	9	2.00
Production-Integrative	2	2	3	4	11	2.47
Research-Sales	4	2	1	2	9	2.51
ERL-Integrative	2	4	2	1	9	2.72
ERL-Production	4	4	4	4	16	2.95

Average Differentiation Score 9.3

Spearman's coefficient of rank correlation for total differentiation and perceived integration (corrected for ties)—.833, which is significant at the .05 level.

* Differentiation Scores
1 = low differentiation
4 = high differentiation

Integration Scores
Lower integration scores indicates more effective integration.

tween the total degree of differentiation and the effectiveness of integration between subsystem pairs (see Figure VI–1). This relationship is significant at the .05 level. Those pairs of units that were most similar in structure and occupational orientation were the ones that the members of the system perceived to have the most effective integration. Those units which were most highly differentiated were the ones which had the most difficulty in obtaining effective integration. Thus, the data at R&P support the hypothesis that within any system there would be a relationship between the degree of differentiation between subsystem pairs and the effectiveness of integration of their activities.

As we would expect, the Integrative unit was less differentiated from each of the basic subsystems than they were from each other. Accordingly, the effectiveness of integration between the Integrative subsystem and the basic subsystems was greater than that between the basic subsystems themselves. The integration scores indicate that the relationships between the Integrative unit and Sales, and the Integrative unit and Research were perceived to be sound, and the clinical data presented earlier substantiated this. The relationship between the Integrative unit and Production also presented no problems, in spite of the high degree of differentiation of the Production unit. As was indicated in Chapter IV, the relationship of the Integrative unit to the ERL, although it permitted effective integration, was not as sound as to the other units. This appears to be attributable to both the high degree of differentiation of the ERL and also to the fact that the Integrative unit was occasionally perceived to be illegitimately initiating activities for the ERL.

At this juncture, it is important to stress an earlier point: that the placement of the linking unit at R&P in an intermediate position not only facilitated its relationship with these basic subsystems, but also contributed to the improvement of relations between the basic units. The Integrative unit seemed to help members of each basic subsystem to have a clearer understanding of the activities of the other basic units, enabling them to develop a greater degree of mutual trust. By improving the flow of both technical information and attitudes, the Integrative unit helped build close ties between the differentiated basic units.

The units at R&P that had achieved the highest level of integration were those linked by the processual integrative devices. This is consistent with our data (Chapter V) indicating that these devices were effective in providing a flow of technical information between units and in developing identification with common objectives.

The only subsystems at R&P that were not joined by a processual integrative device were the ERL and the Integrative unit, and the ERL and Production. We have already presented data about the relationship between the Integrative unit and the ERL, but it might be helpful to examine the relationship between the ERL and Production, since according to the system members, this pair had the least satisfactory integration. These units were the most highly differentiated pair in either system; but this difference was mediated by the presence of the Integrative unit. Although the integration score for these units was the highest for any pair at R&P, our interviews indicated that no serious problems of integration were present at the time of the study. Comments by a scientist in the ERL indicate that differences in subsystem structure and occupational orientation could create problems between these two units, but that they were not creating any serious barriers to the scientific transfer process:

> Historically, the greatest problem has been getting Production to enter wholeheartedly into getting new products out. By the nature of the beast, the production man is conservative. If things are operating satisfactorily, he hates to change them. Production is doing a good job of cooperating now, but this is a recent improvement. Difficulties between research and Production are not unusual. A production man has to look at things differently, because every time he tries something and it goes wrong it costs him profits. Until he understands that if he

doesn't do something his profits are going to disappear, he won't be willing to change readily. But I think that our relations with Production have been working well.

One point on the interface between the ERL and Production where contact was particularly frequent was the pilot plant. It was in this segment of the ERL that processes were tested in larger quantities and modified to meet the demands of full-scale production. The pilot plant manager at the ERL indicated that he, too, felt that there were no major problems in the relationship with Production:

> We have had good relations with production lately. I have seen other situations where production people wouldn't follow the research changes in processes. In [this product group] when we have the recipes outlined, the production people go over them with us and understand them and follow our procedures. At first we had some difficulties, probably because I had to learn what their capabilities were, but now they just sit down with us and we go through the problems and work them out and they follow our recipes.

From this data it seems apparent that even between the most highly differentiated units at R&P there were no serious integration difficulties.

We can draw two major conclusions about integration and differentiation at R&P. First, we have found a relationship between the degree of differentiation and the effectiveness of integration at R&P and this provides support for the first of our hypotheses. Second, we have found that all the units at R&P, in spite of high differentiation between certain units, were able to obtain relatively effective integration of their activities. We shall return to this second point when we compare the two systems.

AT THE CROWN CHEMICAL COMPANY

Our intention was to include all pairs of units at Crown which required high integration in the scientific transfer process. Although the ERL was not as intimately involved in innovation ac-

Figure VI-2—Differentiation and Integration*—Crown Chemical Company

Subsystem Pair	Task Orientation Differentiation	Time Orientation Differentiation	Interpersonal Orientation Differentiation	Structural Differentiation	Total Differentiation Score	Perceived Integration Score
Integrative-Research	1	3	1	1	6	2.76
Integrative-Sales	1	1	3	2	7	2.78
Integrative-Production	1	1	1	4	7	3.10
Research-Production	1	2	1	4	8	3.12
Integrative-ERL	3	4	2	1	10	3.32
Research-Sales	3	3	3	2	11	3.46

Average Differentiation Score $\overline{8.7}$**

Spearman's coefficient of rank correlation for total differentiation and perceived integration (corrected for ties)—.995, which is significant at the .01 level.

* Differentiation Scores
** Adjusted for comparability with pairs at R&P.
1 = low differentiation
4 = high differentiation

Integration Scores
Lower integration score indicates more effective integration.

tivities at Crown as the Research unit, we have included its relationship with the Integrative subsystem in our data because the ERL did play a role in the research activity and because the Integrative unit provided it with information about the market. Crown personnel perceived a need for integration between these units, but not between ERL and Sales or Production. There was also a perceived need for integration between the ERL and Research, but we shall consider this separately when we discuss the ERL's relationship with the Plastic Division in detail.

At Crown there was a strong relationship between the degree of total differentiation within subsystem pairs and the perceived effectiveness of integration of the activities of each pair (Figure VI–2). This relationship was significant at the .01 level. The closer the units were in subsystem structure and occupational orientation, the more effective the role occupants felt they were in obtaining a unified effort. This data also tends to support the first hypothesis.

We also find, as we did at R&P, that the Integrative unit was closer to each of the basic subsystems, than they were to each other. However, as was indicated earlier, the Integrative unit was not completely effective as an integrating device because it was not intermediate between the basic units in structure and occupational orientation. These difficulties in obtaining effective linkage are evident from the fact that the integration scores at Crown were higher for even the least differentiated pair of subsystems than were the scores for all but the most highly differentiated pair at R&P.

The failure of the Integrative unit to obtain an intermediate position is generally reflected in the data in Figure VI–2, but we should note one difference between this data and that presented earlier. In the earlier chapters when data about subsystem differentiation was presented separately for each system, the Integrative unit's failure to be intermediate was quite apparent. In this chapter, however, the data is presented on a single scale which

permits comparison of the two systems. Since the degree of differentiation between subsystems was not as great at Crown as it was
at R&P, some of the differences at Crown do not appear as clearly
here as they did in our earlier data. Nevertheless, that problems
of coordination were being created because the Integrative unit
was not intermediate between the subsystems, is indicated by
both the integration scores (Figure VI–2) and the clinical data
presented earlier. The fact that this was so, in spite of the lower
degree of differentiation between subsystems at Crown, is a matter we will want to return to later.

The influence of the processual integrative devices is not as
clear at Crown as it was at R&P. The data in Chapter V indicated
that the Product Management Committees were not completely
effective as integrative devices. This conclusion is supported by
the fact that the Integrative-Sales pair, which was not linked by
this processual device, was obtaining as much or more of a unified
effort than pairs of units with a similar degree of differentiation
which were linked through these committees.

Thus, the limitations of both the structural and processual
devices at Crown contributed to the fact that there was less effective integration here than at R&P. We have found evidence of
these integration difficulties already, but it might be useful to
briefly explore the relationship between the Sales and Research
subsystems, which was the least satisfactory one at Crown.

This relationship provides us with the opportunity to again
emphasize that the position of the Integrative unit not only influenced the relationship between itself and the basic subsystems,
but also the direct relationship between basic units. The fact that
the Integrative unit was not in an intermediate position between
Research and Sales seems to have created difficulties in obtaining
a unified effort between these units. Both Sales and Research
personnel were concerned about this shortcoming.

A Sales executive stated his opinion about that unit's role in
scientific transfer:

I don't feel that Sales is brought into product evaluation early enough. My feeling is that if we were brought in earlier we could save a lot of time that Research spends working on things. The way things are set up now we are absolutely independent of what is going on with new products. Our only relations with anybody is through [the Integrative unit], but if we were brought in earlier, I think it would help the researchers.

Another Sales executive expressed the view that his unit did not have enough influence in deciding what products were to be worked on:

You always feel out here in the field that you are not getting the degree of cooperation you should. We have been wanting them to work on [a new product] for years. Finally, just this year, they are doing something about it in Research. This program was finally gotten started because a big customer wanted the work done, and [my superior] put terrific pressure on them to get something started. This happened about a year ago. They are still working on the project in Research. The amount of pressure we can put on these things is important. I don't think we have enough influence. If we did we would have gotten this thing done four years ago.

Both of these sales managers, as well as the salesmen working for them, felt that they were having difficulties in getting their appraisals of market conditions to the people who could act on them.

Research personnel also were encountering difficulties in dealing with the highly differentiated Sales unit. A group leader stated his view of the problem in this way:

As a source of market information, the field sales force is so spread out and working on so many things they can't give us good information. They should be a very good source about the primary need, but they aren't. Salesmen come back and tell us about the need in such broad generalities that it sounds like they are talking about super products. They say they would like a clear plastic that can take any color and be completely heat-resistant and be easy to shape. Any idiot knows we all want that but what we need is more specific knowledge coming from qualified persons, such as the salesmen.

This and similar comments pointed to the need for better market information, but other researchers were concerned because the sales force did not appear to be motivated to introduce new products. One group leader indicated his dissatisfaction:

> We lack coordination in getting the new product from the laboratory to the field. It sometimes takes two years to get the field people to push a new product. One thing we have been trying to do is to get the technical person out into the field so that he can push his product himself.

All of these difficulties were attributable to both the Integrative unit's shortcomings as an integrative device, and also to the fact that Sales had no representative on the Product Management Committees. Both factors tended to isolate Sales from intimate involvement in product development.

Although this discussion has concentrated on the relationship between the divisional Research unit and Sales, there was also an inadequacy in the linkage of the ERL to the market. Members of the Crown organization indicated this should be provided through the Integrative unit and not by direct contact with Sales itself. The ERL was working primarily on theoretical problems, and all the scientists interviewed felt that they had too little contact with commercial activities. More contact with the market would have aided them in selecting projects that might have some commercial applications and also would have enabled them to see how they could provide more help to the Plastics Division. A manager in the ERL put it this way:

> We probably should have more contact with the commercial goings-on. It isn't as easy for us to do as it is for the people in Division Research. We have to make a special effort to do it, because there aren't any regular contacts, and there is always something more pressing. It would be helpful to have more commercial contact for us. It would be good not just for me, but for various people at all levels in our section.

Much of the ERL's liaison with the Plastics Division occurred either through the Research subsystem or through Division Management. Although the data indicated that the Research unit and the ERL were not highly differentiated and that they had established a sound relationship, the Research unit was not in a position to provide the ERL with market data, which could stimulate ERL personnel to creatively attack problems created by new market needs. In fact, Research often specified the technical problem to be studied by the ERL and this was a source of some dissatisfaction to ERL personnel.

From this discussion of the relationship between the research units and the units that were in contact with the market, we can see that there were difficulties in obtaining an effective link between the market and research activities. This data supports that presented earlier, in indicating that there were more integration difficulties at Crown than at R&P. Evidence of this also is provided by the relatively higher integration scores at Crown (see Figure VI–2). At Crown as at R&P, we have found that these difficulties seemed to become more intense as the differentiation between subsystem pairs became greater.

Thus, in the two systems we have found support for the first hypothesis:

> Within any organizational system, the greater the differentiation between any two subsystems in relation to the requisite integration, the greater will be the difficulties in obtaining effective integration between them.

Having established that this hypothesis appears to have been valid within each system, and recognizing that Crown was generally having more problems of integration than R&P, the remainder of this chapter is devoted to a comparison of the two organizations.

Subsystem Differentiation and System Performance

The second hypothesis that we desired to test is:

> If other system characteristics are similar, the greater the degree of total differentiation within each system, the greater the problems of integration and the greater the dysfunctional consequences in system performance.

To determine if the data support this hypothesis, we had to examine three variables: the total degree of differentiation within each system, the presence or absence of integration difficulties, and system performance in achieving scientific transfer.

The first two of these variables have already been discussed in some detail. We have found that the R&P subsystems involved in scientific transfer were more highly differentiated than comparable units at Crown. We can find further evidence of this by using the average of the total differentiation scores (Figures VI–1 and VI–2). At Crown the average for the system was 8.7; for the organization at R&P it was 9.3. All the evidence, then, indicates that the R&P system was more highly differentiated than the Crown system. However, our earlier discussions have also pointed to the fact that Crown was encountering more integration problems than R&P. Thus, the less differentiated system was actually incurring more difficulties in integrating subsystem activities. This is contrary to our expectation. Before examining this paradox, we want to present data about the third variable in our hypothesis— the level of system performance.

Obtaining an appraisal of system performance in the development of products is difficult to do. We have, however, attempted to gather empirical measures of the productivity of each system in scientific transfer and have also obtained an appraisal of performance from several executives involved in these activities within each company.

At Crown there was a general feeling among the executives that they had not been as successful in obtaining new and improved products as they could have been. A member of top management stated it this way:

> We are not without new products now, but we just have no overwhelming number of them. One reason we have been unfertile is that we rely too much on the customer's present needs. When you get an idea from them, it is too old. Relying on our salesmen to get ideas from the customer has been fruitless.

A Sales executive also felt that the division was encountering problems in this area:

> We have brought a lot of products out on the market which we couldn't sell. It wasn't that there was anything wrong with the products themselves from a technical standpoint. It was just that when we got them they didn't meet any market need. We didn't have enough evaluation of market requirements early enough.

A Research executive also felt the company was having difficulties in creating new and improved products:

> We are in a pretty poor situation as far as new products are concerned. Fifteen years ago [an older product] was rising rapidly and management saw how profitable it was and put all its eggs in one basket. We didn't worry about new products. The business was profitable but we had no new products to sell. Then we tried [a major new product] but it wasn't profitable. Because of all this we have had no new products left and this has put the squeeze on everybody. I would say that our volume isn't expanding as rapidly as the rest of the industry's and neither are our profits.

These comments indicate some dissatisfaction with the rate of innovation at Crown; however, they do not imply that the division had been completely unsuccessful in introducing new and improved products, but rather that it had not been as successful as some of its competitors. This is also reflected in the per cent of current sales accounted for by new products. In 1963 products introduced within the past five years accounted for 20 per cent of sales. Of this amount over half had been obtained through acquisition or licensing agreements.

The situation at R&P was considerably different. At the end of 1963 products introduced within the last five years accounted for 59 per cent of the sales in the product group with which this study was concerned. These products had been developed internally. Executives indicated this rate would increase during the next year, so that by the end of 1964 it might be approaching 70 per cent. They also indicated that they were quite pleased with this performance. The business manager for this group of products expressed this opinion:

> The thing that is really nice right now is that the fellows in Research and [the Integrative unit] are coming through with new products. This is a dynamic product group. It is really healthy and growing.

A Research executive also pointed to the successes in this group of products:

> I think that our success is based on our ability to work together. We depend an awful lot on faith in each other around here and really in this one product area this past year has been a fantastic success.

The comments of the manager of the Integrative subsystem offer further evidence of the success of personnel involved in this product group in developing products:

> This area has been successful and we have been promoting many of the people in it to other parts of the company. These promotions are the result of wanting to spread some of this talent to other places. We are telling them to go out to these other units and to build up the same kind of team work they have developed in this group of products.

From this evidence it can be concluded that the R&P system was achieving a higher rate of innovation than the Crown system. We, therefore, find a relationship between system performance and integration within the system. R&P, which had fewer problems of integrating subsystem activities, was achieving higher system performance than Crown, which had certain integration difficulties; but we are still confronted with the fact that R&P was the more highly differentiated system. This is contrary to our second hypothesis, unless it can be established that there were differences in system characteristics between the two companies which might account for this ambiguity.

The data have indicated that one factor that contributed to

R&P's obtaining both greater differentiation and better integration was the intermediate position of the Integrative subsystem which placed it close enough to each of the basic units to facilitate its coordinative role. At Crown the Integrative subsystem was not this well placed.

We found in Chapter III that the degree of system structure was greater at Crown than at R&P. Spans of control were tighter, reviews were more specific and more frequent, and formal rules were more central to the task at Crown than at R&P. Another structural characteristic, the locus of formal authority (the level at which decisions could be made), was also different in the two systems. In this study we were primarily concerned with decisions involved in the scientific transfer process, such as those pertaining to the initiation and continuation of research projects and the marketing and processing of new and improved products. The requisites of the scientific transfer process were that these decisions be made at the lower levels of the organization where technical and market data were available. However, there were differences in the locus of formal authority between the two systems. At R&P formal authority for these matters was given to the lowest level of supervision in the Research, ERL, Sales, and Integrative subsystems, and to the Plant Manager who was the lowest executive, in the Production hierarchy, with a comprehensive knowledge of plant matters. The formal authority to make these decisions at Crown was assigned to the laboratory directors in Research, to the department managers in the Integrative unit, and to the plant manager. All of these roles were at a higher echelon than that of similar authority at R&P. On major decisions it was expected that the top management of the division would also be included. The fact that the locus of formal authority was higher at Crown than at R&P is consistent with our general conclusion that Crown had a more structured system than R&P.

We found in Chapter V that the norms of conflict resolution

at R&P indicated that conflict should be resolved by the members of the Goal Teams themselves without depending on superiors. At Crown the norms sanctioned withdrawal from conflict within the committees and reliance upon superiors to resolve conflicts. These norms, operating in the setting of the processual devices, also seemed to be shared throughout each system. Evidence of this can be derived from typical responses to the researcher's question about how conflict was resolved in each company.

The Plant Manager at Crown described how he had been involved in resolving a conflict between one of his subordinates and a Research role occupant:

> Well let's take an example. Two or three months ago I detected that there were too many abrasions between [the individuals involved]. The way I heard this was that we have five or six meetings a month and I sat in on several of them and you don't have to be too perceptive to pick things like this up. I also have good relations with my people and the people out in the lab, so I get these rumblings. When I heard about this thing, I called my boy in and we talked it over. I wanted him and the other fellow to see that each had a side to his argument and that there was some inequity in each position. On other occasions I have called both men in and have gone over it with them together and I tell them, 'You are adults, let's work this out.'
>
> I've also had some differences with [one of the laboratory directors]. Two weeks ago he wrote a letter to the Quality Control Manager about some process changes. The Quality Control Manager was just furious about it. He came in and saw me about it, so I went over to see the laboratory director. The Laboratory Director told me he didn't mean the letter to be a directive, but just wanted to make some suggestions. So I told the two of them to sit down and work it out. They have finally gotten it worked out.

A Research executive also indicated that the norms of how conflict was handled were shared beyond the confines of the Product Management Committees:

> If something submitted by Research isn't ready in [the Integrative unit's] judgment we talk [the Integrative unit] into taking it out to the customer and letting the customer decide what he wants.

The [Research Director] and [the Marketing Director] would be advised that the products need improvement. Of course we can't force anything on [the Integrative unit]. They are Research's customers in the real sense. We have to sell them. Any difficulties we have are brought to the [Research Director's] attention and he will decide if it should receive more attention. He will have a separate meeting with the Research people to thrash it out and this would be the position he presents to [the Integrative unit].

An Integrative executive also indicated that he found it necessary to have conflicts brought to the attention of higher management.

Sometimes when you get into an argument and if it isn't worth it, you let the matter drop, but if it is important then I take steps to get it done, by putting the proposition down on paper with supporting evidence and give them the alternatives. I send this to [the Assistant General Manager]. When he gets the letter, he'll ask the various fellows what they think and he gets results by asking questions. He sort of lets you know that it is important to think about this and this induces people to take action.

From these and similar comments, the conclusion can be drawn that the norms of reliance upon superiors for the resolution of conflict were shared throughout Crown. Their presence in the Product Management Committees was a reflection of shared norms throughout the organization. It should be emphasized that subordinates did not rely on superiors to resolve every conflict, but our data revealed a greater tendency for such reliance at Crown than at R&P.

The norms sanctioning confrontation and working through of conflict at R&P also appeared to have been shared throughout the organization. This conclusion is supported by the comment of a senior research scientist in the ERL:

In my experience, in most cases, these things get worked out with the people involved. I would rarely, if ever, want to go to my boss and ask him to pound somebody over the head for me, because they wouldn't do what I wanted them to. If he did it, it wouldn't be effective anyway. I would feel very sheepish about going to my boss and telling him I couldn't get this thing done. Most of the guys around here are amenable to arguments and persuasion and a few experimental facts.

A similar comment was made by a research administrator in the ERL:

There is only one way our problems [with Production] get worked out. If we feel we are right we keep plugging away, and let time work for us. You have to keep on promulgating ideas until it sinks in. It has to be done with persistence and with the facts. It does no good to get mad and it does no good to give up if you are convinced you are right.

We much prefer that these things be worked out at the level of the people involved. There can be situations where it is necessary to carry it to the people above, but we wouldn't do this unless we were convinced there was no other way it could be handled. I don't mean management shouldn't be informed of what's going on, but I do mean they shouldn't have to be actively involved.

That these norms were shared at the upper levels of the organization is indicated by the Group Sales Manager in describing the inception of the Business Teams:

When we got started thinking about the teams, the only instructions we got were that we, as a Business Team, would be responsible for the long-range profits of this product group. When we first got started, [the Integrative Manager], [the Business Manager], and I really had some arguments about what we should do. I finally suggested that we needed a Research and Production man to help us out. Well, both of these guys argued with me and said they knew enough about those other things and we argued about that for quite a while. Finally, they agreed to go along with it and they had to find a man in these areas. When we first set up the Goal Teams we had the same problems, because nobody told us what the teams should do, but I finally agreed with the others that the Goal Teams should first make long-range plans.

Thus, rather than relying on their superiors to resolve the conflicts about how to set up the teams, the individuals involved worked out the problem themselves.

In both organizations, then, the data point to differences in norms of conflict resolution both in the specific setting of the processual devices and throughout each system.

These norms were related to the formal structure in both systems. One way of conceiving of this is to view the norms as being either legitimate or not legitimate in relation to the system structure. In the two settings studied, a congruence occurred between the locus of formal authority and the norms of conflict resolution. At R&P the level with the authority to make decisions within each subsystem about scientific transfer was also the level that the norms indicated should resolve differences between subsystems. The situation was similar at Crown, although a higher echelon had the sanctions. In both systems, therefore, the norms appear to have been legitimate in relation to the system structure. (We should make it quite clear that we are not implying causality in either direction, but rather are pointing to the fact the norms were legitimate in both systems in that they were consistent with the structure.)

All of these factors indicate, as other researchers have found, that lower system structure is associated with higher system performance in a changing external environment; but we now have a more precise idea about some of the factors that influence this relationship. Our findings suggest that the lower degree of system structure and the norms of conflict resolution at R&P were consistent with the requisites of the scientific transfer process. These factors provided for the resolution of conflict by the roles that had the appropriate technical and marketing knowledge, and thus they facilitated integration. However, at Crown neither the locus of formal authority nor the norms of conflict resolution were appropriate to the requisites of the scientific transfer process that decisions should be made at the lowest level of personnel with the relevant scientific and market knowledge. The structure and norms at Crown specified that these decisions be made at a higher level.

From this study, we can conclude that other factors were not the same in both systems; therefore, we are not able to either support or refute our third hypothesis:

> If other system characteristics are similar, the greater the degree of differentiation within each system, the greater the problems of integration and the greater the dysfunctional consequences in system performance.

Yet the findings suggest that the underlying assumption that greater total system differentiation will be related to greater integration difficulties may be somewhat naive. The proper placement of structural devices and the presence of a system structure and system norms that were consistent with the requisites of the scientific transfer process enabled R&P to attain both higher differentiation and more successful integration. The greater differentiation at R&P was functional for individual subsystem performance, but without the higher degree of integration that was also present, the positive consequences of improved subsystem performance could have been nullified by conflicts between units.

VII
Summary, Conclusions, and Implications

We indicated at the outset that this is an exploratory study in which we are seeking factors that can be investigated further. Yet this study can, even at this point perhaps, provide some tentative answers about the process of differentiation and integration in complex organizational systems. After a summary of these findings, we will consider what implications they may have for the practitioner—both those administering organizations involved in scientific transfer and those in other types of institutions. Finally, we shall briefly consider several questions raised by this study which seem to provide interesting opportunities for future research.

Summary of the Study

POINTS OF DEPARTURE

The prior research and theory taken into account by this study pointed to these major conclusions:

1. The differentiation and integration of basic subsystem tasks were both necessary for effective system performance.

2. Differentiation would also occur in subsystem structure and occupational orientation.

3. This differentiation appeared to be related to problems of integration.

4. Where requisite integration was high, as in the scientific transfer process, integrative devices would emerge to link the differentiated basic units.

On the basis of these prior findings, we developed three hypotheses to be tested:

1. If a structural integrative device is effective in integrating basic subsystems, it will tend to be intermediate between the basic subsystems in structure and occupational orientation.

2. Within any organizational system, the greater the differentiation between any two subsystems in relation to the requisite integration, the greater will be the difficulties in obtaining effective integration between them.

3. If other system characteristics are similar, the greater the degree of total differentiation within each system, the greater the problems of integration and the greater the dysfunctional consequences in system performance.

We also wished to explore the factors related to the effectiveness of processual integrative devices in each system and the influence of differences in system structures and norms on the process of subsystem differentiation and integration. In the process of conducting this research, we also wanted to develop more economical methods of measuring the structure of systems and subsystems and the occupational orientation of subsystem members.

CONTRIBUTIONS OF THIS STUDY

We thus hoped to make three types of contributions—methodological, the testing of hypotheses, and the examination of emergent findings. In addition we recognized that we would be able to confirm or question the findings of earlier research studies.

Concerning methodology, we have developed methods for measuring the task and time orientation of members of various subsystems and, more importantly, have found that it is possible to measure the structural difference between subsystems and between systems. In addition, we have developed at least a crude method of measuring the certainty of the task of various organizational units. All of these methods, admittedly, can be refined and this should be one objective of future research. One area that particularly seems to require further study is the measurement of task and environmental requisites.

In terms of confirming the findings of prior research studies, the basic subsystems, as we expected, were differentiated around their respective tasks in both structure and occupational orientation. We have also found that integrative devices of both the structural and processual type emerged in each system. Further research is needed to learn more about the relationship between the degree of differentiation of subsystems, their task requisites, and their performance. Similarly, future research could be useful in identifying other types of integrative devices.

We have tested our three hypotheses and the data supported two of them. The effectiveness of a structural integrative device appears to be related to its intermediate position in structure and occupational orientation between the basic subsystems it is linking. We have also found within each system that integration effectiveness between subsystem pairs is a function of the degree of differentiation between them. It was not possible to test our third hypothesis about the relationship between differentiation and integration in the two systems because the two systems were not similar in structure and norms.

Nevertheless these differences in system structures and norms have presented us with several interesting emergent findings. First, the effectiveness of processual integrative devices appears to be related to the norms about the locus and mode of conflict resolution. When conflict was confronted and worked through within the setting of these devices, the devices seemed to be functional in integrating the activities of the several subsystems. Second, and equally important, we have found it was possible for one system (R&P) to obtain both higher differentiation and sounder integration, as well as better system performance. This we have related to the intermediate position of the structural device at R&P, to less system structure, and to system norms that sanctioned conflict resolution at the lowest levels of the organization by the mode of confrontation and problem solving. This has suggested that the third hypothesis represents an oversimplification of the relationship between differentiation and integration. Further research is needed to understand the complex relationship between differentiation, integration, and organizational performance; however, on the basis of the findings of this study, we can attempt to make a more comprehensive statement about the relationship between integration and differentiation in complex organizations.

RESTATEMENT OF THE RELATIONSHIP BETWEEN DIFFERENTIATION AND INTEGRATION

We have established that within any one system, holding system norms and structures constant, the effectiveness of integration between any two subsystems is related to the degree of differentiation between them in structure and occupational orientation. We have noted that this relationship holds whether the pair we are concerned with is two basic subsystems or a basic subsystem and an integrative subsystem. This is the rationale underlying the finding that the effectiveness of an integrative unit is related to its intermediate position between the units it is intended to link. By being intermediate in structure and occupational orientation, the integrative unit is in the optimal position to coordinate the activities of the several basic subsystems. If the integrative unit is more similar to one of the basic units, it must be less similar to other basic units, and this impairs its ability to obtain unity of effort with these units.

We have also found that another variable, the norms of conflict resolution, is related to integration in the system. Integration within the system is related, then, to the total differentiation between the basic subsystems, the location of the integrative subsystem in relation to its requisite location, and the norms of conflict resolution.

Before considering the relationship between integration and system performance, we should emphasize again that, although we did not attempt to measure systematically the influence of differentiation on subsystem performance, prior research has indicated there is a relationship between the differentiation of a subsystem around its primary task with appropriate structure and occupational orientation and subsystem performance. Thus, subsystem performance is a function of the subsystem's actual location in structure and occupational orientation in relation to its task requisites.

Recognizing this, we can go on to state that system performance is not only a function of integration but also of the performance of the individual subsystems. The validity of this relationship is suggested by the fact that R&P, which was achieving higher performance, had not only more effective integration, but also greater subsystem differentiation in structure and occupation orientation which appeared to be more appropriate for high subsystem performance. We originally expected that a greater total degree of differentiation within the system would be related to more integration problems and dysfunctional consequences for system performance. But we have found that a system can obtain higher differentiation without sacrificing unity of effort between its parts, through the effective use of structural integrative devices and by having a degree of system structure that is appropriate to the requisites of its task and that facilitates integration in the setting of processual integrative devices.

We have presented in this discussion a more concise restatement of the relationships between subsystem differentiation, integration, and system performance to which the findings of this study point. Although these findings are somewhat tentative, they do suggest certain implications for the practitioner.

Implications for Administrators

The setting in which this study was conducted represents, in a sense, the worst of all possible worlds for the administrator, since the several subsystems involved require a high degree of integration, but are also highly differentiated, varying from a short-range, process oriented, highly structured production subsystem to a long-range, research oriented, low structured research subsystem. In comparison to other industrial settings, both the degree of differentiation and the degree of integration required are higher, and the administrator in this setting is constantly confronted with the difficulty of obtaining some balance between the two.

Although the implications of this study may have particular relevance to executives in firms involved in scientific transfer, they are a major issue in most organizational settings and should have general practical significance. Whether the firm is a department store with the perennial problem of integrating the activities of merchandising and operating units, or a consumer products manufacturer with the need to integrate sales and production units, these same issues are present to some extent.

One important implication of this study—that the structure of a large organization is not necessarily homogeneous—has already received some attention in recent literature.[1] Different sub-systems should and, according to our findings, often do have different degrees of structure depending upon the requisites of their tasks. Similarly, we have found that different occupational orientations are appropriate for different tasks. Therefore, a manager confronted with the problem of administering a highly programmed factory will find more structure, and a more directive interpersonal orientation as well as a short time orientation and production task orientation, appropriate for his organization; whereas the research administrator concerned with organizing the creative activities of a laboratory of scientists will find that more structure, a more permissive interpersonal style, a longer time orientation, and a research task orientation are more functional for the performance of this organizational element.

While research findings have been pointing to the functionality of this differentiation, popular management literature has tended to treat structure and interpersonal orientation as being based on principles that are widely applicable regardless of the particular task and other situational factors; thus, we have had books outlining principles of organization and administration and large firms have tended to apply homogeneous organizational structure throughout their diverse parts.

One example of this tendency was evident at Crown where corporate management tended to standardize structure. As a consequence certain units at Crown were not appropriately structured for their task. On the other hand at R&P, where the structure in each subsystem had evolved more naturally in relation to its particular task, we found structure was more consistent with unit task. We are not implying that some firms are completely undifferentiated, but rather that there has been a failure on the

1. For example, see H. J. Leavitt, "Management According to Task: Organizational Differentiation," *Management International,* I (1962), pp. 13–23.

part of management and many management theorists to recognize the need for differentiation around individual subsystem tasks.

The tendency to seek broad principles that can be applied to all situations can also be seen in the fact that the findings of social scientists have often been interpreted as being applicable to all situations. For example, there has been a tendency in recent years to regard "participative management" as a panacea for any situation. We now have arguments about whether "theory X" or "theory Y" management is more appropriate. The question is: More appropriate for what? The implication of our findings should be clear: Different structures and different occupational orientations are appropriate to different tasks. The problem confronting the administrator is to ascertain the specific task requisites of the various subsystems within his organization and then to consider what structures and occupational orientations are appropriate to each part. By doing so, he should be taking a long step toward greater organizational effectiveness.

Regardless of whether subsystems are appropriately differentiated around their individual tasks, our findings indicate that differentiation will be present in the system, so that the administrator must also be concerned with integrating the differentiated subsystems. The relationship that we have found to be present between differentiation and integration within any one system provides a useful operational method of examining the problems of obtaining integration between units. In a system confronted with integration difficulties, an analysis of the differentiation in structure and occupational orientation will tend to highlight some of the factors related to these difficulties. In this sense, then, we have provided a diagnostic tool for examining these problems.

Beyond this, however, the study has also provided some useful leads about structural design, or redesign, once these problems have been identified. We now have some notion of what makes a structural integrative unit effective. If an investigation of integration problems within a system indicates that they are related to a high degree of differentiation between two units that have high requisite integration, our findings provide some data about what the requirements would be for an effective structural device designed to link these units.

As an example of how this might work, we can place ourselves in the role of the top management of the Plastics Division at Crown. Our analysis has indicated there were integration problems between both the Research and Sales units, and the Research and Production units. This difficulty seemed to be partially related to the fact that the Integrative unit was not in an intermediate position in structure and occupational orientation. Specifically, we found that it tended especially to be too highly oriented toward short time concerns and not sufficiently concerned with plant and scientific matters. Thus in attempting to alleviate these difficulties, management should establish at least two objectives—to balance the time concerns of the Integrative unit and to increase its concern with plant and scientific factors.

With these objectives clarified, management would then have to turn to the complex issues of how these changes could be implemented, given the intricate fabric of the social system which is the Integrative unit. In this study we have not been concerned with the issues of change, but we will shortly want to consider the relationship of this study to problems of obtaining organizational change and will return to this point.

So far we have been concerned with the degree of differentiation and the problems of integration within one system, but this study, as well as earlier ones, have indicated that total systems may have different levels of structure, depending upon their total organizational task. Whereas there is a need for differentiation between subsystems in structure, total systems can have more or less structure overall. This was clearly demonstrated by the differences in system structure between R&P and Crown. Crown appeared to have more structure in all its subsystems than similar subsystems at R&P.

Perhaps the most significant findings from this study related to this difference in system structures is the importance of different norms of conflict resolution which seemed to be legitimatized in each system structure. Since the process of differentiation creates different norms and cognitive states in the various subsystems, there will always be some conflict between representatives of different units about how to proceed. Conflict will exist and it must be handled. The effectiveness of the integration of the activities of the different units is a function of the manner in which conflict is dealt with in the system. If it is confronted and resolved, as it was at R&P, conflict can be functional in that it provides an opportunity to explore the various ideas and factors involved in any decision. The dysfunctional consequences are minimized, since conflict does not become a disruptive force in the system. If it is avoided and passed on to others for resolution, it can have a more disruptive effect on system performance. This seemed to be demonstrated by the situation at Crown.

Two points that should be emphasized are that confrontation and working through of conflict appear to be necessary for effective integration within any organization, and that the appropriate locus of conflict resolution depends upon the requisites of the organizational task. Given the tasks of the firms in this study, we have pointed to the need for resolution to occur at the lower levels of the organization where the complex market and technical factors were well understood. In other settings, however, it might be appropriate for conflict to be resolved at higher levels of the organization. For example, in an organization that is mass producing one uniform product, it might be consistent with the organization's task to have conflict about a product change resolved at the upper levels of the organization where information about the total national market and about the impact upon all production facilities would be available.

One factor at Crown which we have found working against the attainment of conflict resolution in this manner was the system structure. The higher degree of structure legitimatized withdrawal from conflict at the level where the task requisites indicated it should have been resolved. At R&P, however, the system structure seemed to reinforce confrontation of conflict at the lowest levels of the organization. Since the structure and norms seemed to be so intertwined, in both systems, this raises several related questions. How could Crown management intervene to make the mode and locus of conflict resolution more consistent with the task requisites? Would structural changes bring this about? Is there some other way in which these norms can be changed?

The question of organizational change is not the central focus of this study; yet the problems of achieving meaningful change in an organizational system are closely related to some of the important implications of this research. For this reason it seems fitting to consider briefly these questions, emphasizing particularly the relevance of this study to the issue of changing organizational behavior. As we do so, we can consider not only the problem of changing the mode and locus of conflict resolution, but also the issue raised earlier of changing the norms and cognitive states within an integrative unit, such as the one at Crown.

As Lawrence has pointed out in an earlier study, there are several methods available to bring about changes in organizational behavior patterns. These include the influence of peers, superiors, and subordinates; formal training devices; and structural changes. Lawrence concluded that a combination of methods is often appropriate. He referred to this as 'the cookbook approach.'[2] In our current discussion, we would like to concentrate on a recipe which includes two of these methods—formal training devices and structural change. In recent years the use of

2. P. R. Lawrence, *The Changing of Organizational Behavior Patterns* (Boston, Harvard Business School, Division of Research, 1958), pp. 204–205.

small training groups to bring about changes in interpersonal behavior, norms, and values has received increasing attention. The
findings of this research have significance in relation to this work.

Blake and others have recently described one attempt to influence the values and norms of members of an organization
through the use of instrumented task groups.[3] Argyris reports
some success in changing interpersonal behavior through the use
of sensitivity training.[4] Without dwelling on the differences between these methods or their relative merits, we can point to one
conclusion which seems to be shared by the several people working in this area. This is the fact that for the behavioral changes
that result from the use of these training devices to become per-
manent, it is necessary to bring about changes in the structure
of the organization consistent with what the participants have
learned through the training sessions. Argyris makes this point:

> Laboratory education is not a panacea, nor is it a process that can
> help every organization. Furthermore, it must be accompanied by
> changes in the organization, its policies, managerial controls, and
> even technology. Not all organizations can profit from it; nor do all
> organizations need similar amounts of it. All of these factors should
> be carefully considered before becoming involved.[5]

If one of the objectives of a training session is to attempt to
alter the behavior of organization members so that they are more
likely to confront conflict and work it through, it might also be
necessary to make changes in the structure of the organization, so
that when the participants attempt to apply their new behavior
pattern in their 'back home' organization, they will find that the
structure actually reinforces the behavior rather than making it
illegitimate.

3. R. Blake, et al., "Breakthrough in Organizational Development," *Harvard
Business Review*, XLII (November–December 1964), pp. 133–155.
4. C. Argyris, *Interpersonal Competence and Organizational Effectiveness*
(Homewood, Richard D. Irwin, 1962).
5. C. Argyris, "T-Groups for Organizational Effectiveness," *Harvard Business
Review*, XLII (March–April 1964), pp. 72–73.

The present study points to one particular element of system structure that it is especially important to modify if an organization is seeking to alter the norms of conflict resolution. This is the locus of formal authority for decision making. We have indicated that in both organizations the locus and mode of conflict resolution seemed to be particularly related to the locus of formal authority. For management to hope to achieve any success in obtaining the resolution of conflict at lower echelons, it would be necessary to delegate some of its prerogatives for decision making to those lower levels. To emphasize the complexity of the interrelationship between norms and structure, we should also note that it is not necessarily a simple matter for an upper management group accustomed to making decisions to delegate this authority to subordinates. This involves a change in norms of behavior just as fundamental as that required of personnel at the lower echelons who are being asked to accept the resolution of conflict as a legitimate activity at their own level.

Returning to the questions raised earlier about how Crown management might intervene to bring about desired changes in behavior, we suggest at least two possible methods. First, training devices might be useful to bring about changes in norms and cognitive states not only in relation to conflict resolution, but also perhaps in relation to the problem of altering the behavior of members of the Integrative subsystem. But Crown management would also have to make certain changes in the structure of its organization. These might include changes in the formal locus of authority and a redefinition of the activities of the Integrative unit so that a different time and task orientation would emerge which is consistent with both its integrative function and the other instrumental tasks it is performing. Changes such as these would enable the system's integrative devices, both processual and structural, to function more effectively.

The implications of this study which seem most significant for practitioners are, first, that managers should clearly recognize that effective organizational performance requires that organizational systems be differentiated in both subsystem structure and occupational orientation. But this differentiation is related to difficulties in obtaining effective integration, which is also necessary for organizational effectiveness. Therefore, our findings about the conditions under which integrative devices are effective are also important. If structural integrative devices are intermediate in subsystem structure and occupational orientation, they will facilitate integration. The effectiveness of processual devices is related to the norms of conflict resolution present in the wider system. These, we have found, are related to differences in system structure that are appropriate to different task requirements. If a system is structured appropriately for coping with its environment, this will also facilitate integration by legitimatizing norms of conflict resolution consistent with the demands of the task. Finally, we have pointed out that the findings of this study can be helpful to managers interested in changing organizational behavior patterns to obtain more effective integration. Changes in behavior through training devices must be accompanied by corresponding changes in system structure if they are to be lasting, and this study has increased our understanding of the structural characteristics that are functional for effective integration.

In conclusion, we must again emphasize that the central problem confronting the administrator is to obtain a balance between differentiation and integration within the system. It is not necessary to give up differentiation to achieve integration. The effective functioning of structural and processual integrative devices will permit both higher differentiation and more effective integration and will allow the organization to reap the benefits of high performance. That this ideal state of affairs is attainable has been demonstrated by our findings at R&P.

By pointing to some of the factors related to the effective performance of integrative devices, and by more precisely defining the relationship between differentiation and the effectiveness of integration, this study should contribute to the administrator's understanding of the conditions underlying the attainment of an optimal balance between differentiation, which enables the basic subsystems to cope with their respective environments, and the integration of their activities, which is also essential to effective system performance.

Now needed is more knowledge about the complex relationship between differentiation and integration, the organization's tasks, and organizational performance. Further research is necessary to clarify the relationship between subsystem structure and occupational orientation, subsystem task requisites, and subsystem task performance. It might also identify other dimensions along which organizational units are differentiated. Work is needed to understand the emergent findings about the norms of conflict resolution, so that we can know more about the conditions that enable some organizations to develop effective modes of resolving conflict whereas others do not.

These are only a few of the questions that this research has provoked for us. They are suggestive of the many opportunities open to social scientists who are willing to accept the risk of working with tools that are still imperfect and with concepts that have not been fully tested in order to take the small steps which, when totaled, may measurably increase our understanding of man's behavior in organization.

Methodological
Appendix

Both analytical and clinical methods were used to collect data. Because of the few operational tools for measuring the
organizational variables with which this study is concerned, one
of the objectives in undertaking it has been to develop at least
some crude analytic measurements of the relevant variables. At
the same time, we recognized that it would be necessary to rely
on clinical interviews and observations of meetings to conduct the
more exploratory aspects of the study and to provide a deeper
understanding of the process of differentiation and integration
in the two systems.

The analytic data were collected through the use of a questionnaire given to 85 respondents in both organizations and from
organizational documents and interviews with executives about
structural and environment characteristics in both companies.

The clinical data were collected through interviews with the
same 85 informants and through the observation of meetings in
both companies. In the selection of informants an attempt was
made to reach all of the role occupants involved in the scientific
transfer process in each subsystem. In both companies there were
more persons directly involved in scientific transfer in certain units
(especially research) than in others (for example, production or

sales); therefore, more informants were obtained from the former units than the latter. Even so, because of the large number of persons involved in scientific transfer in research units, it was possible to interview and question only a sample of persons at the lower echelons.

This discussion of methodology will first consider the analytic methods used to measure each of the variables we are concerned with; then it will briefly describe the clinical methods used to collect the additional data.

Task Requisites

We have attempted to hold the environmental factors confronting both systems constant by selecting two organizational systems in the same industry. However, each basic subsystem has a different task with different requirements; we expected these different tasks to be related to differences in subsystem structure and occupational orientation. To test whether or not the subsystems in this study were appropriately differentiated in relation to their tasks along these two dimensions, some understanding of the task requisites of each unit was necessary. Determining the requisite task and time orientation did not present any particular problem, but it was necessary to develop a method of measuring the task requirements that we would expect to be related to subsystem structure.

Studies have been cited which indicated that structure would be related to the degree of certainty of the task. The more programmed the task, the higher the degree of structure that is functional for task performance. To state more precisely what determines the certainty of the task, it is first necessary to make a distinction between the environment and the task. As we have indicated, each subsystem must cope with a particular segment of the environment. The subsystem task, then, is really a strategy developed to deal with the environment. The certainty of the task is related to at least two environmental factors: the certainty of information in the environment and the rate of change in the environment. A third factor, which is part of the task itself, is the primary time span of concern of the subsystem.

The certainty of information refers to how well documented facts are in the environment at any point in time. The second factor refers to how rapidly these facts are changing. The time span of concern influences the certainty of the task, because firm information for some future period is usually more difficult to establish than it is for the current one. By conceiving of certainty of the task in this manner, we are attempting to establish more precisely the factors in the task and the environment which other researchers have found are related to structure. The scale that has been used to measure these three elements of task certainty is presented in Figure A–1.

Figure A–1—Task Certainty Criteria

Certainty of Information	Rate of Change	Primary Time Span	Score
Few established facts	Constant change	1–5 years	1
Knowledge of general facts	Moderate change	3 months–1 year	2
Knowledge of detailed facts	Change occurs infrequently	1–3 months	3

Structural Characteristics

At the outset of this study several sets of structural characteristics, which other researchers and authors had suggested might be fruitful for examining differences in organizational structure, were available. Evans had proposed one set in a recent article.[1] Pugh and his colleagues had suggested a somewhat similar set.[2]

1. W. M. Evans, "Indices of the Hierarchical Structure of Industrial Organizations," *Management Sciences*, IX (April 1963), pp. 468–477.
2. D. S. Pugh et al., "A Conceptual Scheme for Organizational Analysis," *Administrative Science Quarterly*, VIII (December 1963), pp. 289–315.

Burns and Stalker, in describing their organic-mechanistic typology, also outlined the characteristics they had used to distinguish between the two types.[3] Finally, we have already mentioned the structural elements that Hall used in his study.[4] These authors have indicated that high structure is characterized by more specific goals, procedures, and rules; a greater number of levels in the hierarchy; tighter spans of control; and shorter time spans of responsibility.

Even with these leads in the structural dimensions that might be relevant for our purposes, we were still confronted with the problem of defining them operationally, since few of the prior researchers had made any attempt to measure them operationally. Confronted with this difficulty, we elected to develop our own set of characteristics, basing it on those suggested in the prior literature as far as this was operationally feasible. The characteristics used are listed in Figure A–2, along with the criteria used to de-

Figure A–2—Structural Characteristics Utilized

	Low Structure	High Structure
Average span of control	Wide	Narrow
Number of levels of hierarchy	Few	Many
Time span of review of subsystem performance	Long	Short
Specificity of review of subsystem performance	General	Specific
Centrality of formal rules	Peripheral to task	Central to task
Specificity of evaluation of role occupants	General	Specific
Locus of formal authority for decision making	Low echelons	Upper echelons

termine their position on the continuum between low and high structure. All the characteristics with the exception of the locus of formal authority have been used to compare subsystem structures as well as system structures. The locus of formal authority was not used to compare structural differentiation between sub-

3. T. Burns and G. Stalker, *The Management of Innovation* (London, Tavistock Publications, 1961). See especially pp. 119–122.

4. R. H. Hall, "Intraorganizational Structural Variables," *Administrative Science Quarterly* (December 1962), pp. 295–308.

systems because, operationally, differences did not exist on this dimension.

To compare the total degree of structure between subsystems or between the two systems, four-point scales for each of these structural dimensions have been developed (see Figure A–3).

Figure A–3—Scales of Structural Characteristics

Scores (From Low ⟶ High Structure)

Structural Characteristics	1	2	3	4
Average Span of Control	11–10	9–8	7–6	5–3
Number of Levels in Hierarchy	7	8–9	10–11	12
Time Span of Review of Subsystem Performance (Based on shortest review period).	Less frequently than once each month	Monthly	Weekly	Daily
Specificity of Review of Subsystem Performance	General oral review of performance	General written review of performance	One or more general statistics	Detailed statistics
Centrality of Formal Rules	No rules	Rules on minor routine matters	Comprehensive rules on routine matters and/or limited rules on operations	Comprehensive rules on all routine matters and operations
Specificity of Criteria for Evaluation of Role Occupants	No formal evaluation	Formal evaluation— no fixed criteria	Formal evaluation— less than 5 criteria	Formal evaluation— detailed criteria—more than 5

Although these scales do not cover all the possible dimensions of structural differentiation, they do provide a measure of structure that is operationally feasible.

Occupational Orientation

The second major variable along which we expected subsystems to be differentiated was occupational orientation in its three dimensions: interpersonal orientation, task orientation, and time orientation.

Fiedler's *Least Preferred Co-worker Scale* has been used to measure interpersonal orientation (see Figure A–4). This semantic

Figure A–4—Instrument for Measuring Interpersonal Orientation
Least Preferred Co-worker*

People differ in the ways they think about those with whom they work. This may be important in working with others. Please give your immediate, first reaction to the items on the following page.

On the next page are pairs of words which are opposite in meaning, such as Very neat and Not neat. You are asked to describe a person with whom you have worked by placing a check in one of the eight spaces on the line between the two words.

Each space represents how well the adjective fits the person you are describing, as if it were written:

Very neat: ____ : ____ : ____ : ____ : ____ : ____ : ____ : ____: Not neat

8	7	6	5	4	3	2	1
Very neat	Quite neat	Some-what neat	Slight-ly neat	Slight-ly un-tidy	Some-what untidy	Quite untidy	Very untidy

FOR EXAMPLE: If you were to describe the person and you ordinarily think of him as being quite neat, you would put a check in the second space from the words Very neat, like this:

Very neat: ____ : __x__ : ____ : ____ : ____ : ____ : ____ : ____: Not neat

8	7	6	5	4	3	2	1
Very neat	Quite neat	Some-what neat	Slight-ly neat	Slight-ly un-tidy	Some-what untidy	Quite untidy	Very untidy

Look at the words at both ends of the line before you put your check mark. Please remember that there are no right or wrong answers. Please do not omit any items and mark each item only once.

Now, think of the person *with whom you can work least well.* He may be someone you work with now, or he may be someone you knew in the past.

He does not have to be the person you like least well, but should be the person with whom you had the most difficulty in getting a job done. Describe this person as he appears to you.

1. Pleasant	:__:__:__:__:__:__:__:__: Unpleasant
	8 7 6 5 : 4 3 2 1
2. Friendly	:__:__:__:__:__:__:__:__: Unfriendly
	8 7 6 5 4 3 2 1
3. Bad	:__:__:__:__:__:__:__:__: Good
	1 2 3 4 : 5 6 7 8
4. Distant	:__:__:__:__:__:__:__:__: Close
	1 2 3 4 : 5 6 7 8
5. Supportive	:__:__:__:__:__:__:__:__: Hostile
	8 7 6 5 : 4 3 2 1
6. Contented	:__:__:__:__:__:__:__:__: Discontented
	8 7 6 5 : 4 3 2 1
7. Stubborn	:__:__:__:__:__:__:__:__: Not stubborn
	1 2 3 4 : 5 6 7 8
8. Not enterprising	:__:__:__:__:__:__:__:__: Enterprising
	1 2 3 4 : 5 6 7 8
9. Tense	:__:__:__:__:__:__:__:__: Relaxed
	1 2 3 4 : 5 6 7 8
10. Not studious	:__:__:__:__:__:__:__:__: Studious
	1 2 3 4 : 5 6 7 8
11. Unsympathetic	:__:__:__:__:__:__:__:__: Sympathetic
	1 2 3 4 : 5 6 7 8
12. Impatient	:__:__:__:__:__:__:__:__: Patient
	1 2 3 4 : 5 6 7 8
13. Happy	:__:__:__:__:__:__:__:__: Depressed
	8 7 6 5 : 4 3 2 1
14. Unenthusiastic	:__:__:__:__:__:__:__:__: Enthusiastic
	1 2 3 4 : 5 6 7 8
15. Not confident	:__:__:__:__:__:__:__:__: Confident
	1 2 3 4 : 5 6 7 8
16. Disagreeable	:__:__:__:__:__:__:__:__: Agreeable
	1 2 3 4 : 5 6 7 8
17. Unproductive	:__:__:__:__:__:__:__:__: Productive
	1 2 3 4 : 5 6 7 8
18. Unadventurous	:__:__:__:__:__:__:__:__: Adventurous
	1 2 3 4 : 5 6 7 8
19. Sociable	:__:__:__:__:__:__:__:__: Unsociable
	8 7 6 5 : 4 3 2 1
20. Satisfied	:__:__:__:__:__:__:__:__: Dissatisfied
	8 7 6 5 : 4 3 2 1
21. Unambitious	:__:__:__:__:__:__:__:__: Ambitious
	1 2 3 4 : 5 6 7 8

Reproduced by permission of Fred Fiedler, Department of Psychology, University of Illinois.

Figure A–5—Questions Used to Measure Task Orientation

In evaluating and considering the potentialities of a new idea, there are many considerations about which persons in different parts of the organization must be concerned. We recognize, while all of these concerns are important, that at the stage at which you become involved in the innovation process certain concerns will be most important to you. In order to learn which are most important in your personal opinion we would like you to rank the 10 criteria listed below as follows:

a) Place a "1" by the three criteria which are of most concern to you personally.

b) Place a "2" by the *next four criteria* which are of *second most* concern to you personally.

Criteria:

_____The manufacturing costs associated with products resulting from the proposed idea. (Plant)

_____Competition's response to products resulting from the proposed idea. (Market)

_____The potentialities for scientific publication which might result from the proposed idea. (Scientific)

_____The return on investment which the company might gain from the proposed idea. (Company-wide)

_____The technical processing problems which might result from the proposed idea. (Plant)

_____The contribution which research on the proposed idea might make to scientific knowledge. (Scientific)

_____The capability of the sales organization to sell a product resulting from the proposed ideas. (Market)

_____The plant facilities which would be required for a product resulting from the proposed idea. (Plant)

_____The technical capability of the research staff to conduct research on the proposed idea. (Scientific)

_____The effect of products resulting from the proposed idea on the sales of existing company products. (Market)

Note on Scoring Method

First choice criteria were weighted one, second choices were weighted two, and those not selected were weighted three. Thus, the lower the combined score on all the criteria for a certain environmental sector, the more concern the individual (or subsystem) indicated for that task concern. The data presented have been arranged for each unit, so that units can be compared on this three-point scale.

differential scale asks the respondent to describe a co-worker with whom he has had most difficulty working. Although Fiedler has been using this instrument to measure leadership styles, it can also be used to provide data about general interpersonal orientations along the dimensions of directive versus permissive types.

The assumptions underlying the criteria used to measure task orientation (see Figure A–5) were that each basic subsystem would be oriented to some degree toward one of the three segments of the system's environment—the market, the scientific environment, or the plant environment. Three criteria were included for each segment. A tenth criterion dealt with company-wide concerns but was not used in the analysis of results since it did not distinguish between subsystems.

The time orientation of the various subsystems was measured by using the question presented in Figure A–6. Four possible time orientations are delineated in the question; however, those dealing with one month and one quarter were combined during our analysis into short time concerns. Middle-range time concerns were considered to be between three months and one year, and long-range concerns have been treated as one to five years.

Figure A–6—Question Used to Measure Time Orientation

What per cent of your time is spent working on matters which will show up in the division profit and loss statement within:

a. 1 month_____
b. 1 quarter_____
c. 1 year_____
d. 5 years_____

Note on Scoring Method

One month and one quarter have been combined as short-range, within one year is middle-range, and within five years is long-range.

	Scientific Orientation		Market Orientation	Plant Orientation	Total Difference in Task Orientation
Sales	2.7		1.2	—	
Research	2.0		2.4	—	
Difference	.7	+	1.2	=	1.9

As a first step in scoring the differences in structure and occupational orientation, the differences between each pair of subsystems were determined for structure and for each element of occupational orientation. This presented no problem for structure or for interpersonal orientation, since each unit had a single structural score or average LPC score. However, for task and time concerns it was necessary to follow a somewhat more complex procedure, since there were three different possible orientations in both task and time concerns.

In summarizing task orientations, the difference in the criteria with which the units had a mutual requisite concern was computed for each pair of subsystems. Then the total of those differences was obtained and was used as the difference in task orientation for that unit. To illustrate this, we can use a pair of subsystems from R&P, the Sales and Research units. These two units had a mutual requisite concern with scientific and market matters, and therefore the difference in plant concerns was not considered.

Thus for these two units the total difference in task orientation was scored as 1.9.

In measuring time orientation, the differences between each pair of units in short-, middle-, and long-range time concerns were computed and these were then totaled for that pair. The same pair of units from R&P provides an example.

	Short Range		Middle Range		Long Range	Total Difference in Time Orientation
Sales	48		36		16	
Research	23		48		29	
Difference	25	+	12	+	13	50

Having computed these differences, the range of difference *in both companies* was divided into four classes and scored on a four-point scale. These scores and the range of differences are presented in Figure A–7.

Figure A–7

Score	1	2	3	4
Difference in Structure Scores	0–1	2–3	4–5	6–8
Differences in Interpersonal Orientation (LPC)	0–8	9–17	18–26	27–35
Difference in Task Orientation Scores	.5–.8	.9–1.2	1.3–1.6	1.7–1.9
Difference in Time Orientation Scores	9–42	43–76	77–110	111–144

Integration Effectiveness

A second major variable to be considered is the effectiveness of integration obtained between subsystems. Ideally we would like to have measured this by considering the actual unity of effort obtained between units; however, this is operationally difficult, if not impossible. Instead we have relied on the perceptions of members in the various subsystems about the effectiveness of integration achieved between the various unit pairs (see Figure A–8). Members were asked to rate all possible relationships between these pairs because, at the time the questionnaire was devised, we had not yet established which pairs had high requisite integration. Once this was determined our analysis was focused on the appropriate subsystem pairs. We also relied on data from clinical interviews to obtain an evaluation of integration effectiveness. This will be discussed in more detail below.

Figure A–8—Question Used to Measure Integration Effectiveness

This question is aimed at obtaining your evaluation of relations between units within the company involved in innovation (new products, product improvements, new processes, etc.). The list at the right contains statements which describe the state of the relationship between two units. Select that statement which you feel is most appropriate for each set of relationships and enter the corresponding number in the square provided below.

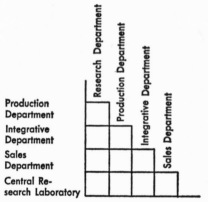

Relations between these two units are:
1. Sound; full unity of effort in obtaining innovations is achieved.
2. Almost full unity.
3. Somewhat better than average relations.
4. Average; sound enough to get by even though many problems of achieving joint effort on innovations.
5. Somewhat of a breakdown in relations.
6. Almost complete breakdown.
7. Couldn't be worse; bad relations; serious problems exist in getting innovations which are not being solved.
8. Relations are not required.

Note:

The responses were scored on the same seven-point scale respondents used in making their evaluation.

It should be noted that this question was altered slightly for each company, depending upon the actual nomenclature used for departments. The example shown here includes all departments, but in the analysis only those with high requisite integration were included.

System Performance

The system performance in which we were interested is the achievement of scientific transfer; this includes both new products and the further development of existing ones. It is difficult to obtain any measure that completely describes a company's performance in these activities, but we have selected one criterion which provides an approximate measure of system performance— i.e., the per cent of total product sales represented by products developed in the last five years. In addition to this empirical measure we have also gathered clinical data from the executives in each system about their perceptions of the system's effectiveness in developing products.

Clinical Data

The analytical methods just described provided most of the data required for this research; however, we recognized that the exploratory nature of this study made it important to use interviews and observations to gather additional data about the systems under study.

The interviews were generally about one hour in length and usually followed the outline of questions presented in Figure A–9.

Figure A–9—Interview Questions

1. As a starting point could you tell me how decisions actually get made on new projects? For example, whom do you talk to about starting and stopping projects; whom do you consult about getting more people or additional funds and equipment; and how frequently are these projects reviewed?

2. In working on these matters how much direction do you receive from your superiors; is this direction sufficient or would you like more direction or less? For example, does your boss give you specific instructions about how to carry out activities or does he leave the details up to you? Do you consider his comments to be instructions which must be followed or as suggestions which may be disregarded?

3. How many persons outside your unit do you come into contact with frequently —say, once a week or more—while you are working on innovations?

4. I would like you to rank the various functions (sales, production, and research) in terms of their general standing in the company. That is, which units do people in the company (or division) consider to have the highest and the lowest standing?

5. I would now like to spend a little time talking about the coordination of the several units involved in the transfer process. Before we talk about how the various segments work together, I would like to get your thoughts on where close coordination is most important. Could you rank each set of units in terms of the closeness of coordination required to obtain effective action on innovation projects? (List units and work through the ranking with respondent.)

6. Which of these units initiate most of the innovation ideas? What other units are required to follow through on these ideas?

7. In meetings with representatives of different units about new product matters, how frequently do you have disagreements?

8. What is the nature of these disagreements and what positions do the representatives of each unit take?

9. If there are disagreements which are difficult to resolve, do you continue discussions until a solution is reached or do you ask for help from a higher authority?

10. What committees, liaison individuals and other devices are used to improve coordination between your unit and other units? I would also like to get your opinion about the strengths and limitations of these devices.

11. How do all these things add up in terms of your feelings about your job and career?

On occasion, however, when the informant had interesting data about a particular aspect of the situation, these interviews dealt in more detail with that topic. These interviews were usually treated as diagnostic interviews in which the researcher and the informant shared data (to the extent they were not confidential) and their significance. This does not imply that we attempted to advise informants on how to handle their problems; rather we sought to deal with them as professional equals with whom we could share ideas about organizational phenomena.

In addition to the interviews, we observed several formal and informal meetings in each company to gather data about the effectiveness of various processual devices. Our strategy in observing the conduct of the meetings was to maintain an 'open' posture, so that we could gather data about those characteristics that might be related to the effectiveness of their performance as integrative devices.

Name Index

Argyris, C., 160

Barnard, Chester, 5, 19
Barnes, L., 2n, 14, 15
Bavelas, A., 8
Blake, R., 160
Booz, Allen, and Hamilton, 20
Brown, Wilfred, 7
Burns, T., 10, 20, 22, 168

Christie, L., 8

Dearborn, D., 17
Dickson, W., 2n

Evans, W. M., 167

Fiedler, F., 12, 170–173

Hall, R. H., 11, 168
Homans, G., 1n
Hower, R., 2n

Lawrence, P. R., 11, 18, 159
Leavitt, H. J., 8, 11
Luce, K., 8

Macy, J., 8
Mayo, Elton, 5
McClelland, D., 16
Miller, 19
Miner, J., 16

Orth, C., 2n

Pugh, D. S., 167

Rice, A. K., 2n, 6, 12, 19
Roe, Anne, 15–16
Roethlisberger, F., 2n
Ronkin, H., 17

Seiler, J., 18, 18–19
Sheperd, H. A., 2n
Simon, H., 17
Spencer, Herbert, 4
Stalker, G., 10, 20, 22, 168

Trist, E. L., 2n
Turner, A., 11

Woodward, Joan, 9

Subject Index

Allport-Vernon Study of Values, 15
Authority, delegation of, and decision-making, 161
  and organizational structure, 168–169

Behavior, changes in organizational, 159–160, 161–162
  differences in occupational, 14–17
  and norms, in organizations, 1–2, 7
  relation of, to structure, 10
Business Team, at Rhody and Procter Chemicals, 90, 92

Committees, as processual integrative devices, 20, 89
Conflict resolution, 158–159
  and delegation of authority, 161
  and integration, 153
  and processual integrative devices, 151–152
Crown Chemical Company, 35, 36, 39–42
  basic subsystems in, 39–40, 52–62
  compared with Rhody and Procter, 62–64
  differentiation and integration in, 133–139
  integrative subsystem in, 76–88
  interpersonal orientation in, 56–57, 80
  major roles in, 40
  processual integrative devices at, 92–94, 110–125

structural integrative devices at, 76–88
  subsystem structure scores for, 54, 56, 79
  task orientation at, 59, 60, 80–81, 82
  time orientation at, 59–61, 81, 83

Decision-making, and authority, 161
Differentiation, definition of, 1
  dimensions of, 7–18
  earlier research on, 4–7
  and integration, 18–23
  problems of, 3
  see also Subsystem differentiation

Environment, changing, as complex organizational task, 10
  stable, as routine organizational task, 10
  and structure, 10, 22
Executives, differences in perceptions of, 17
  functions of, 5
  implications of study for, 154–163
  perceptions of organizational effectiveness of, 176–177

Exploratory research, as basic subsystem, 37, 39

Goal Teams, at Rhody and Procter, 90–92, 95–110, 121–125

Innovations, structural integrative devices as, 20

Instrumented task groups, and organizational change, 160
Integration, definition of, 1
  devices to achieve, 20–22
  and differentiation, 18–23
  effectiveness, measures of, 175–176
  problems of, 3
  requisite, and interdependence, 19
  research on, 4–7
  and structure, 22
  and subsystem differentiation, 128–139
Integrative devices, 20–22
  effectiveness of, 162
  processual, 20–22, 89–125
  structural, 20, 21, 64–88
Integrative subsystem, as linking basic subsystems, 21
Integrative subsystem (Crown), 76–88
  and basic subsystems, 78–83
  effectiveness of, 83–88
  functions of, 76–78
Integrative subsystem (Rhody and Procter), 66–76
  and basic subsystems, 68–72
  effectiveness of, 72–76
  functions of, 66–67
Interdependence, and differentiation, 19
  see also Integration, requisite
Interpersonal orientation, 12–14, 17, 18
  at Crown, 56–57, 80
  measures of, 170–173
  at Rhody and Procter, 48–49
Interviews, as clinical data, 177–178

Kuder Preference Record, 16

Leadership, measures of, 173
  and task performance, 12–13
Least Preferred Co-worker Scale, 170–171
Liaison specialists, 20

Management Committee, at Crown Chemical Company, 93

Methodology, 150–151, 165–178
  analytical, 165–177
  and clinical data, 177–178

Norms *see* Behavior; Values

Occupational groups, values among, 14–18
Occupational orientation, 7
  definition of, 12
  and different tasks, 155–156
  dimensions of, 12
  measures of, 170–175
  in plastics industry, 47–51, 56–61
  see also Interpersonal orientation; Task orientation; Time orientation
Organization, behavior in, 1–2, 7
  implications for change in, 159–163
  nonhomogeneous structure of, 154–155
  processes in, 5–7
  as a socio-technical system, 1–2
  structural characteristics of, 167–169
  subsystems in, 6
  values in, 14–18
  see also Crown Chemical Company; Product Innovation, and organization; Rhody and Procter Chemicals

Perceptions, about effectiveness of integration, 128, 129, 176–177
Plastics industry, 25–34
  basic subsystems in, 27–29
  environment of, 25–26
  requisite integration in, 29–34
  see also Crown Chemical Company; Rhody and Procter Chemicals
Processual integrative devices, 20–22, 89–125
  comparison of, in two companies, 121–125
  and conflict resolution, 151–152
  emergence of, 90–94
  functioning of, 94–121
Product innovation, and organization, 1

conclusions for, 149–150
and criteria for selecting organizations, 34–36
focus of study on, 1
and hypotheses tested, 150
implications for, 154–163
methodology of study on, 150–151,
165–178
research setting for, 25–42
summary of study on, 148–154
Production, as basic subsystem, 7
in plastics industry, 28–29
Product Management Committees, at
Crown Chemical Company, 93–94,
110–121, 121–125

Research, as basic subsystem, 7
in plastics industry, 27
see also Exploratory research
Research setting, criteria for, 25–42
organizations chosen for, 34–42
and requisites for scientific transfer
process, 25–34
Rhody and Procter Chemicals, 35–39
basic subsystems at, 37–38, 43–52
compared with Crown Chemical, 62–
64
differentiation and integration in,
129–133
integrative subsystem at, 66–76
interpersonal orientation at, 48–49
major roles in, 38
processual integrative devices at,
90–92, 95–110, 121–125
structural integrative devices at, 66–
76
subsystem structure scores for, 46,
48, 68
task orientation at, 49, 50, 70
time orientation at, 49–51, 71

Sales, as basic subsystem, 7
in plastics industry, 27–28
Scientific transfer process, 1, 25–34
and basic subsystems, 27–29
conceptual diagram of, 31

definition of, 1
and environment, 25–26
and problems of differentiation and
integration, 3
requisite integration for, 29–34
Sensitivity training, and organizational
change, 160
Social system, processes in, 4–5
Structural integrative devices, 20, 21,
64–88
at Crown Chemical Company, 76–88
at Rhody and Procter, 66–76
Structure, and organization, 1–7
changes in, 160–161, 161–162
characteristics of, 167–169
comparative scales for, 169
relation of, to task performance, 8–12
Subsystem differentiation, 4ff.
basic divisions of, 7
at Crown Chemical Company, 52–62
and integration, 128–139
around primary tasks, 6
at Rhody and Procter, 43–52
and system performance, 139–148
System performance, and effectiveness
of integration, 23, 128, 153–154
measures of, 176–177
and subsystem differentiation, 139–
148

Task, relation of, to structure, 8–12
at Crown Chemical Company, 52–62
at Rhody and Procter, 43–52
Task certainty, 27–29
at Crown Chemical Company, 53
measures of, 151, 167
at Rhody and Procter, 45
Task orientation, 12, 13–14, 17, 18
at Crown Chemical Company, 59,
60, 80–81, 82
measures of, 151, 172, 173
at Rhody and Procter, 49, 50, 70
Task requisites, 166–167
need for measures of, 151
Task specialization, 1
see also Subsystem differentiation

Teams, as processual integrative devices, 20, 90
Technology, and organizational structure, 10
Time orientation, 12, 13–14, 17, 18
at Crown Chemical Company, 59–61, 81, 83

measures of, 151, 173
at Rhody and Procter, 49–51, 71
Training devices, and organizational change, 159–160, 161, 162

Values, occupational, 14–18

About the Author

The author, JAY WILLIAM LORSCH, is Assistant Professor of Organizational Behavior at the Harvard University Graduate School of Business Administration. He received the B.A. from Antioch College, the M.S. from Columbia University Graduate School of Business, where he was a Samuel Bronfman Fellow in Democratic Business Enterprise, and a Doctorate of Business Administration from the Harvard University Graduate School of Business Administration, where he was a Ford Foundation Thesis Fellow. During 1964–1965, he was Research Fellow in Business Administration and member of the faculty at Harvard.

This publication under the Arkville Press imprint was set on the Linotype in Caledonia, with display in Monotype Bulmer; printed and bound by The Book Press, Brattleboro, Vermont. It was printed on paper supplied by S. D. Warren Paper Company. The colophon was created by Theodore Roszak.